tripping with jim morrison
& other friends

MICHAEL LAWRENCE

with an introduction by
TIMOTHY LEARY

blackbird

This edition published in 2016 by

Blackbird Digital Books
2/25 Earls Terrace
London W8 6LP

www.blackbird-books.com

First published as 'Jim & I' in the USA by iUniverse (2003). All rights belong to the author

ISBN 978-0-9933070-3-4

Copyright © Michael Lawrence 2016
The moral right of the author has been asserted

All rights reserved. Except in the case of brief quotations quoted in reviews or critical articles, no part of this book, word or image, may be used or reproduced in any manner whatsoever (electronic, mechanical, photocopying, recording, or otherwise) without the prior written permission of the above publisher of this book.

A CIP catalogue record for this book is available from the British Library

Cover and interior bronze portrait of Jim Morrison by Michael Lawrence
Height: 25 inches 1980 Private collection, Ca.
All illustrations c. Michael Lawrence
Cover design by Nuno Moreira www.bookcovers-design.com

This book is dedicated to all the treasures of the imagination

"You have poems inside your head and you have learned to explode them with firecracker tubes of paint"
Ray Bradbury

"The guys from your UCLA days sent me your way, claiming your memories and stories of Jim are among the most important"
Jerry Hopkins (Co-author of the Jim Morrison biography No One Here Gets Out Alive)

"I won't try to compete with you in the word department except to say how much I enjoy reading yours."
Roy Lichtenstein

Table Of Contents

Introduction
1. Pancakes with Jim and Mom   1
2. Blake's Little Lambs   9
3. Poem for a Helicopter   14
4. View From my Dashboard   28
5. Clay Portraits and Judy Garland   33
6. Salvador Dalí at the Seaside   39
7. Descending the Staircase with Duchamp & Jean Harlow   43
8. Peace Pipe   48
9. Ten Year Old Antique   51
10. Chaplin and Other Early Heroes   55
11. Behind a Curtain of Flannel Pyjamas   61
12. Tripping with Jim   68
13. Poetic Ammunition   78
14. Self-Realization Center   83
15. Working with the Boys   89
16. Spilt Popcorn   92
17. Boudoirs of Young Girls   99
18. Adventures with Don Quixote   107
19. Magical Dancing Trees   110
20. Beauty and Genius   116
21. Endless Bazaar   123
22. Plumtree's Potted Meat   129
23. Shuttlecock   137
24. The President's Analyst   144
25. Living Inside a Gaudí Building, Casa Milà   148
26. Candlelight on Nixon   152

27. A Dalí Dream, Soft Time   155
28. Cauliflower Opera   160
29. The Three Ring Circus   170
30. Powwow with Jim   175
31. The Mirror Without a Face   178
32. I Spent a Kiss Dreaming   183
33. Paris, Let Me Swim in Your Streets Forever   185
34. Turner, Fuckin' Turner   191
35. Les Deux Magots   199
36. Walking into a Paul Klee World   204
37. Rocky Raccoon   210
38. Readymade Planet   215
39. A Passport for Jim Morrison   222
40. There are No Goodbyes   226
Coda   229
About the Author   230
Further Reading   233
Reader Ambassadors   235

A Forward by Timothy Leary

The 60's in America was different and difficult for all of us. It was a time of fast thinking, profound shifts of direction, and a lot of fun. The Doors of Perception were glued together by many souls. And, we had in common a need for mutual dignity, freedom, and passion.

This story is about a young man at 20 under the influence of art. He is in rebellion with his parents, Hollywood, America, and the Arts. Growing up in Europe, meeting history on the walls of the Etruscan frescos, walking the Tiber, and finding the fountains of Rome erotic and funny prompted his first calling to become an artist. His parents were artists in the film world. They were sympathetic to Michael's odyssey. His picture of the eternal city was transposed from a Hollywood upbringing.

The book begins in Venice, California on an L.S.D. trip with Jim Morrison, who is also looking for his identity. Their friendship helps define each of their paths. Michael's world view, like Jim's, tries to be hip. Where Michael's optimism fails he finds his bravery and his imagination. The world feels in flux and his affection for people and their art forms become his faithful companions.

I identified with this naivete. The riddle of life has several options, and Michael has the time to sort out his lot. He is lucky. We can study his boyish charm at leisure. I wonder if many young people today have the time to consider their privileges. Michael owes his parents a part of the freedom he explores.

This is a sweet story which suggests that ultimate resolutions may not be the answer. This is no surprise. However, here is a wealth of impressions! People, places and events, famous and personal sit side by side in curious metaphors, that softly draw the reader into meditation.

This Lawrence trip catches something of this passion or faith and the landscape of the 1960's. It is, as a book, an interesting guide to a path we are now returning to. 'Sight and setting,' or the organizing of how to view reality, effects how we see the wonderment of creation itself.

The sight and setting focus around art provides subtle shifts that are illuminating, pleasurable, and often funny. An adventure of rich feelings and a sense of human growth evolves.

The book ends with the word, "go."

Timothy Leary
July, 1990

INTRODUCTION

The 60s in America was different and difficult for all of us. It was a time of fast thinking, profound shifts of direction, and a lot of fun. *The Doors of Perception* were glued together by many souls. And we had in common a need for mutual dignity, freedom and passion.

This story is about a young man at 20 under the influence of art. He is in rebellion with his parents, Hollywood, America and the Arts. Growing up in Europe, meeting history on the walls of the Etruscan frescoes, walking the Tiber, and finding the fountains of Rome erotic and funny prompted his first calling to become an artist. His parents were artists in the film world. They were sympathetic to Michael's odyssey. His picture of the eternal city was transposed from a Hollywood upbringing.

The book begins in Venice, California on an LSD trip with Jim Morrison, who is also looking for his identity. Their friendship helps define each of their paths. Michael's world view, like Jim's, tries to be hip. Where Michael's optimism fails he finds his bravery and his imagination. The world feels in flux and his affection for people and their art forms become his faithful companions.

I identified with this naïveté. The riddle of life has several options, and Michael has the time to sort out his lot. He is lucky. We can study his boyish charm at leisure. I wonder if many young people today have the time to consider their privileges. Michael owes his parents a part of the freedom he explores.

This is a sweet story which suggests that the ultimate resolutions may not be the answer. This is no surprise. However, here is a wealth of impressions! People, places and events, famous and personal, sit side by side in curious metaphors that softly draw the reader into meditation.

This Lawrence trip catches something of this passion or faith and the landscape of the 1960s. It is, as a book, an interesting guide to a path we are now returning to. 'Sight and setting', or the organising of how to view reality, affects how we see the wonderment of creation itself.

The sight and setting focus around art provides subtle shifts that are illuminating, pleasurable and often funny. An adventure of rich feelings and a sense of human growth evolves.

The book ends with the word, 'go'.

Timothy Leary
July 1990

1

Pancakes with Jim and Mom

I am a voice, an experience at Jim's grave. They will be coming to find the spot, the James Douglas Morrison spot, so tightly wedged between the stones. The tourists are like hounds, they can smell the odour of Proustian roses. If I'm in an expansive mood I'll bring along flowers and some incense but it is enough for me to bring my bronze. My portable memorial portrait, my James Douglas Morrison. It is not that heavy; it affords me light exercise. I have rented a room near the cemetery and when the weather is good, I lug out my bronze and place it atop a neighbouring stone so that it peers down as if Jim were looking at his own grave. His fans are not content with it alone, they want to know how we darted about like two flickering spirits in the grey afternoon, the warm drizzle, the milkwood path, the adventure story.

Bronze! How it glows in the afternoon. No need of spirits. The sunlight never bleaches a word from the sculpture. I have to supply that. One important thing is not to appear too anxious. As far as that goes I am happy for the air and the peace and quiet of the place. It feels as if I have virtually moved in. Some days I will bring my typewriter along. I have found a spot not too far away from this hub of activity that permits me some peace of mind. Very important for the serious artist!

I have written reams of stories in the company of varied geniuses who have never minded my presence. Often their spirit will add a touch or two. Baudelaire is good for that! I'm glad he has not lost his critical sense entirely.

Morrison, on the other hand, seems to be forever restless, poor dear. He does, however, approve of my presence and he gets a big kick out of his bronze mask, which is now providing a living for me. I made this bronze for Jim. I wanted to have it installed at his grave. Carrying it back and forth makes me a vendor of tales; the bronze face welcomes his admirers and adds grace to his resting place. His grave is an unattractive, cramped space.

My arrangement with posterity is not as grandiose as the tomb of Oscar Wilde. There is a great deal of space around the small building that houses his remains, but it is only since my presence at the cemetery that his tomb is noticed. I have a certain affection for the works of Mr Wilde as well, whose own vanity, a faith in beauty and knowledge, destroyed his health and brought to a short conclusion a life that had been so rich in poetic invention. Certainly I shall have to weave a tale wherein these lost souls gather to compare their lives' battle against the constraints of social behaviour. Modigliani, a beautiful young Italian, came to Paris and painted his nudes with such sensual richness that his only solo exhibition was closed by the police the day it opened. He died of drink, hashish and as the contemporary expression goes 'life in the fast lane'. He was thirty-six. His mistress leaped to her death upon learning of his demise.

Even after death their accomplishments are not always safe from vandalism. Oscar's tomb was designed by the American sculptor

Jacob Epstein who fled America for England. But he did not escape my admiration, his carving of a winged figure, a floating Babylonian pagan god with an erect penis provided Mr Wilde with an appropriate carriage to the afterlife. This penis, his magic wand, was knocked off...so you see, even in memory he continues to be emasculated, misunderstood. This winged creature of Mr Wilde's transported my feelings to his fairytales, so remarkable in their detail, his knowledge of gems and flowers were like a flight of affection...for children. This is what Jim's grave required, a poetic touch. My story is drifting, forgive me! I am merely trying to show that it was through affection for Jim that I wrote to his parents. I enclosed a photo of my memorial portrait; it was the first version I had made. It was an attempt to create the mask of his face when it had been lean, sculpted by the use of LSD at the zenith of his sexy days. Jim's gift was that he could make reality intimate and public at the same time. He took a clear cultural step forward, a song made in current history. The sculpture that I would actually present to his parents I had reworked, adding some of the fatigue of continually being in the spotlight on the train to fame. The expression matured, the face filled out.

Jim's parents agreed to come to see my sculpture at an exhibition I was having. It was the unveiling of this version. They would come early. I went to greet them in the parking lot. His father, Steve, a thin frail man moved with the same grace I first noticed in Jim's walk. I imagine Jim also inherited his sense of strategy from his dad who had been an admiral during the Vietnam conflict. Clara, Jim's mom, thrusting her bosom forward with the air of authority, followed me and led her husband into the gallery. I sensed it was from her, ironically, that Jim's reserve of strength to rebel had blossomed. They had marched in rapidly and, having quickly glanced at the bronze from a distance, they announced their verdict.

"This is not Jim." Clara Morrison spoke with anger. She shot a look to her husband. "This is not my son!"

"Is this the same sculpture? The photo you sent was different."

"Yes, it is a new version, I'd hoped that you would like it. But, if you prefer..."

"Well, we don't like this one, it is not our Jimmy."

The idea that the bronze could be changed hadn't penetrated the shock of seeing this one.

"This is not the same sculpture you sent us a picture of, am I correct?" The admiral wanted to know if he had the story straight. It was as if I had betrayed them. I had only wanted to surprise them with the 'Jimmy' they had in mind. That was the only time I ever heard anyone call him 'Jimmy'.

I wasn't able to reassure them, tell them I'd do another version, because they rushed out almost in a panic. The admiral placed a map on the hood of his car and asked me in a distant tone of voice as if I were a stranger, did I have any recommendations on the best way to get out of Pasadena. I went over to examine the map, but Mrs Morrison became impatient and ordered her husband into the car. I hid my disappointment out of respect. There was a brief symbiotic feel to the admiral's request, like wanting to get close to Jim through his friend who was also an artist. I think he felt guilty for not spending more time with Jim, growing up as he did under his mother's domineering spirit.

Alone for a moment, knowing I'd have to face my parents who would want to know Jim's parents' reaction, I felt robbed of the pleasure of the unveiling of my new sculpture. My mother also liked the first version better. She had commented that Jim's eyes had a quality of looking out and in at the same time. That hadn't changed. The angelic, androgynous, innocent expression, which was a passing phase, was what everyone wanted the boy-angel who sang *Light my Fire* to be.

My mother knew Jim as a college student, a young polite guy in khaki pants studying film at UCLA. She had made us pancakes one morning. She understood by his natural cool manner a form of intelligence. She liked him immediately; this pleased me, and gave her a chance to tell some of her stories. She could be the centre of attention as we had the house to ourselves. My father was away, busy with a film. We were used to entertaining ourselves when he was away. My mother was a writer. And so was Jim. I had my notebooks as well.

"Do you know the work of Paul Bowles?" My mother pulled from the air.

"Ah, he lives in Tangiers, writes about foreigners, how they are changed in Morocco removed from the familiar, other behaviour comes into play."

"Perfecto!" Mom put her thumb to her forefinger, signalling that Jim had hit the bull's eye. This was not surprising, as Jim had taken a course in set design in high school. He had conceived of using a spotlight, which would grow bigger as the play *Cat on a Hot Tin Roof* by Tennessee Williams unfolded. The growing light was to symbolize the growing cancer inside of Big Daddy, the patriarchal figure whom everyone wanted to please. Tennessee Williams was a popular celebrity in the early 60s. Paul Bowles had done the music for his plays and it was known that he wrote. The 'beats': Kerouac, Ginsberg and Burroughs, had visited Paul in Tangiers. This scene is also familiar to young people interested in avant garde literature.

"We threw a party for Tennessee in Rome, in the early fifties. Has Michael told you of our stay in Italy?"

"I didn't go into Paul Bowles, Mom." I had liked Jim's idea for the play, but I hadn't told him about my mother or that she wrote plays.

"Paul brought the hashish." My mother liked to shock. Jim uncrossed his legs and looked into the hazel eyes and pixie face that had addressed him. "The Sirocco wind was blowing that night. We had a large terrace and the gathering included many old friends: Richard Basehart and his beautiful Italian bride, Valentina Cortese, who was a star then, and Paul had a few friends, and of course Tennessee Williams. The warmth of the Sirocco can put you into a trance, get under the skin, make you crazy. It is an unpredictable force."

Jim's head had tilted and it was clear that my mother had an audience. She liked to paint moments and took her time selecting the colours.

"All at once Ten's laughter would cackle through the air. We were smoking hashish in cigarettes, which had an effect like the wind, unpredictable. Large eucalyptus trees across the street swayed, their leaves made a rustling sound. They looked like strange gigantic creatures, rattling our subconscious with vague suspicions. Under the influence of our smoking, the occasional passing car added a kind of B-movie element of suspense. Basehart, who had been sitting next to Valentina holding her hand, got up for a drink to quiet his nerves. He had recently finished a film for Fellini which hadn't as yet been released. My husband was jumpy. He wanted to play the lead in the film Richard was discussing, Fellini's next project, *La Strada*. Basehart was fond of Marc. My husband's desires can be overwhelming. It is his intensity. He knew he would be perfect for the part that eventually Tony Quinn played."

Jim nodded. My mother's voice had slipped into a southern accent giving her description a theatrical touch.

"Tennessee was playing a game with Richard, suggesting that sex appeal was a fragile commodity; like perfume it could evaporate or drive people away. He can be a little devil, that Tennessee. He was clever never to suggest that Dick had a problem, but with the hashish and Paul's Moroccan friend who was wearing a burnoose, a surreptitious atmosphere was created. Tennessee was reading fortunes, looking at the cards. Then abruptly his laughter would break loose. It's a high-pitched hyena's cry, electrifying. 'For Christ's sake Tenny, write me a play and stop torturing, Dick,' my husband said in a menacing tone.

"Tennessee released another volley of laughter, pleased with himself." My mother was smiling, recalling the night. "I wrote a play in the next two days. I couldn't sleep, it poured out."

Was Jim fascinated? We were familiar with the dreamy realities of grass. I had heard the story. She had told it well for Jim.

"Michael smokes in his room, I can smell it. He listens to that terrible Indian music," she shot me a glance of 'oh well' and faced Jim. "Do you enjoy smoking that rubbish?" Her statement was in odd contradiction to the benefits she had just spoken of but there was no tone of malice to her voice, rather a sort of bemused acceptance of youth's experimental period.

Jim was gazing out the window. He turned, smiled and then addressed my mother speaking slowly. "It's research. Sometimes I write a lot under the influence, I can be happy to watch what is happening around me... it changes the point of view. You look at yourself looking. That is what is neat. You look at yourself looking and so what you observe is something which you are also creating. It's kind of... what I think Wittgenstein said about observing reality, that it responds to your looking like a whistle a guy gives to a pretty girl; reality is winking back at you or winking because you are looking at it." Jim was smiling and then he added, "I'd like to read your play." I was glad he had sidestepped what is a boring subject of conversation.

"Well, it's another kind of game now. I don't know... read it!"

"I like the forces you play with Mrs Lawrence. I'll write down my observations for you to read." Jim wasn't trying to be presumptuous, he merely wanted to put his scholarly side to some use and mom was pleased by his offer.

"I think that would be fine, but it isn't necessary to address me as Mrs Lawrence. We aren't that formal around here."

My mother began to talk about her own youth. She had taken her own father to court because he had thrown her boyfriend out of the house. Edward Dahlberg, a writer, was several years older and he wrote about the sexual habits of animals and insects and their strange affection. My mother had secretly married him. She was a bohemian herself.

"Well, Mrs Lawrence, I'm real pleased I've discovered a new friend."

My mother laughed at Jim's over-playing at being polite.

"You know Jim, I can remember being three years old... I found a jar of cherries soaked in liquor. When my father Noah came back, he found me sitting on the kitchen floor, schicker... you know, drunk. We both started to laugh."

There was a pleasant pause in the conversation.

"Ah, I guess we should be going," Jim said.

"I wrote a novel about this period."

"Was your novel ever published?" Jim asked at the door.

"It was optioned for the movies, but sadly the war came and it was never made. *Ask No Return*. I have it somewhere, but read my play, it's much more contemporary."

"I'll look after it." Jim held it close. "Thank you again for the pancakes and the lovely conversation." Jim politely extended his hand. We walked to the garage and to my car. I could tell Mom had really enjoyed talking to Jim. He was a good listener. I think it was also neat for Jim, a hip mom, with whom he could be himself. Of course how is one to know all of this if I don't tell you? But then who is to say if the differences of our upbringing didn't also give us something in common and focused us to go our different ways? But I won't talk about that part first. The important thing is that we fell into life's tavern and knew we had mutual friends even if they existed mostly in books.

2

Blake's Little Lambs

I have spent my life alone, filled with sensation, privilege and pleasure—to that inheritance I salute and respect my parents and all the happy thoughts, alive in the ever-expanding cosmos of my mental universe.

The tourists would be arriving at Jim's grave. Poets take up the paintbrush, words conjure spirit, paint puts it on the tongue. It helps to appear a touch mad under these circumstances. I have to be careful, however, not to scare them off. To lighten things up, I throw in bits and pieces of *Tropic of Cancer*. The important thing is to keep their attention. And to be graceful about collecting funds. Sometimes I say that it is for the Blake Society. This is indirect enough so that they never think of themselves as having been taken. It is easier for them to give to Blake than to me. I would merely be throwing away more money buying tubes of watercolour and luscious Arches papers upon which I paint. I've got a knack for painting, they say. Well, I've been doing it a while. I can remember my gluteus max falling quite asleep whilst I diligently rendered a quaint façade round the corner from Campden Hill Square. That's when I was living in London, going for long walks, learning to smoke a fag or two. The atmosphere there was invigorating after living amidst the soft orange terracotta colours and flowing feel of Rome. London sharpened my sense of life with cool steel grey tones and the crisp angles of her architecture.

In London I saw the film *Moulin Rouge* about Lautrec by Huston, *The Horse's Mouth* by Alec Guinness and *Lust for Life* starring Kirk Douglas.

After three continuous years in Rome, to hear English spoken everywhere was a thrill, a luxury. I read *White Hunter, Black Heart* about John Huston in Africa with Humphrey Bogart making a film. My dad had worked for Huston in *Asphalt Jungle* and so I wanted to be up to date with my dad's world. I had no time for school; I painted street scenes sitting on the curb feeling the hard realities of suffering for my art, becoming a painter, a sculptor, and a storyteller. These were my passions. Seeing the lives of three artists was too much of an experience not to get moving on my own development. To supplement my income, I worked selling antiques with an older lady at a flea market. I discovered that I could buy subway tickets with antique coins at a fraction of the real price. I tried to turn in my tickets for real cash. The police did not approve of my ingenuity and I was taken to the station with my father where I pledged to discontinue my brokerage firm. I have never stayed in any one place long enough to become thoroughly part of it. Often, when people meet me they are hard pressed to guess where I am really from. It never suits them to learn that I was born in California, but they let it go in the interest of hearing all the details of my adventures with Jim Morrison. The format is simple: in life you become a star or his friend. The story may make a good movie. The problem with movies is that they often miss the full literature of life, the sequence of thoughts behind the actions.

   My father is an actor, a cinema character actor who makes the stars look good. That is the way it was in the 1930s when, leaving New York and the theatre, he bummed his way to Hollywood. Character actors were eventually typecast and my father's face, which is well known, having appeared in 178 films more or less, eventually became recognizable as the gangster who stood by Bogart. He was in the original Dillinger gang. Indeed he was once mistaken for Dillinger, and was held at gunpoint in Kansas, until he proved he was an actor, not the true Dillinger. Growing up I wasn't permitted to see him in the movies because his presence was brutal and menacing and so I always imagined him to be someone like Hopalong Cassidy, a hero, one of the good guys, just as all dads are heroes in their sons' eyes until that critical point when they fall from grace and become people. In fact, I may have been a teenager before I actually saw him in a film: *Key Largo* with Bogart and Edward G. Robinson and a ravishing Lauren Bacall. I saw the film for the first time on TV when I was fifteen, living with my mother and uncle and aunt. My father wasn't there, he wasn't always around. When I was four or five I developed eczema and asthma, nervous disorders as I missed the warm tones of his voice, which used to tell me stories. Paco, the wise donkey, who could answer all questions, was the Aristotle of my youth. When Paco wasn't available I made up my own stories, like the giant wolf that lived in the backyard and guarded my safety. Being near-sighted, I listened carefully for his special signals. And there was my cat as well. We got up one morning and discovered a sea of large spiders in the den, so I just stepped on them. I hated being alone; I learned to manoeuvre my crib into the living room down the hallway. I was even younger then.

Oh, for a grain of understanding! What was Morrison to me or I to him, that I weep these crocodile tears? How to express muted adoration, how to express joy… throwing his legs around my waist. For whom is this memory? For what purpose? But the thought that there is purity, that we were Blake's little lambs, makes all this research worthwhile. Are you getting lost in my storytelling? Don't worry, it is I who am jumping around. Don't be annoyed by this, take what I say in good faith. My story is being presented surrealistically by the atmospheres I feel I should show you before you begin to put the puzzle together. Perhaps it's a way to create an LSD experience without the drug? It doesn't matter where I am, only the sequence of my thoughts. Come on, come on, follow them, you'll be OK. I won't abandon you. Watch your own thoughts happening, looking in my mirror. You may sometimes fall into it and come out the other side, where reality has its own logic, a different bridge of association, the view more psychological than chronological. Why something happens seems more interesting to me than when, but it is all an excavation site: the treasure may last only a fleeting moment. Well, let us continue with the narrative.

Am I a coward?

Who pulled out the drugs and threw them in my face? I'd rather not say that I took those drugs… but that would be a lie, and when all is said and done did they not give me back the truth, an understanding of myself and my fellow man? "Don't hit that plant." "Be kind to yourself, Harry." Do you know that Allen Ginsberg gave a radio interview at the Plush Pup, a hot dog stand on Sunset Strip, or that Carol danced on the rooftop at Lenny Bruce's funeral gathering, which was held impromptu at a tract home nearby because the cemetery people did not trust us to behave?

In the 60s I collected my poets' souvenirs, discovering the talents and imaginations of other rebels. They seem more courageous than myself, confronting the world as they did face-on, taking a stance and chirping from their own platforms. I had no experience of Ginsberg's poem, *Howl*, yet I wanted to see his pain, sense what that experience had been. It was frightening to think, to feel that void, that lack of security. Painting and writing somehow filled that space with something concrete. It's not so bright and cheery to dig up the past, more fun to explore into the future. I met Jim Morrison in Holmby Park near UCLA. He was starring in a student film. It was 1964, a warm day, I saw him in the distance standing on a hill listening to the director. He collected his stance between pure attentiveness and lazy musing. With it all, never a sloppy gesture. He fainted for them with great style, passing out in the mode of a great and graceful conductor, bidding adieu to the last sound of the orchestra like a Zen monk stopped in meditation. So easy for him to have the girls come running.

3

Poem For A Helicopter

Jim was cute; he didn't have to say very much. I was born a month and a day before him; we were the same age. He showed me his notebooks by reading from them. He had a small apartment on the second floor in Westwood, on Goshen Avenue. There were several collages on the walls, figures in space that gave a feeling of great distances and sunlight.

"Whose collages?" They were neatly put together.

"Mine," Jim answered softly. "Ah, let me read you something, okay?" He was distracted, anxious to share something with me.

"Sure." He disappeared into his closet. I peeked over his shoulder. There were no clothes, just books and papers.

"Where are your clothes, man?"

"On my back," Jim responded shyly. I didn't laugh. I flashed onto a guy I remembered from camp in Switzerland. He had worn the same clothes for three months; I always wondered how he kept them so clean.

"Sit down, I'll be right out." As I pulled out a chair from his kitchen table, I noticed a print of a Francis Bacon painting. The Pope dissolving in a booth.

"You like Bacon's work?" Jim didn't answer. I liked the aesthetics of joy better.

I liked paintings that gave pleasure. But I wasn't going to argue about aesthetics; I was happy just to have the company of a fellow outsider. I wanted to see what Jim had to offer. He had some papers in his hand.

"Let me read you something. It's short." He sat down and looked at me. I was ready.

"As violet dawn wings are placed
TV races me over the sea
I have played with the Gods in darkness
A calculated risk
Teenage girls shake pompoms in the sunlight.
I will die a hero in their eyes."

Jim looked up, slowly.

"I like it," I said firmly.

Jim wasn't satisfied, he looked at the paper and let it drop, floating to the table. He got up and went to the door. Outside he began climbing up a ladder. I followed. Above was a small roof terrace exposed to a vast expanse of blue sky.

"I like being up here next to the sky," Jim mused.

A police helicopter appeared. Jim became excited. He started running around the terrace like an Indian on the warpath. He was shooting imaginary arrows at the helicopter. When the copter disappeared Jim turned off his act.

"When did you write that poem?" I asked. Jim began calling to an imaginary dog.

"Hey, fella, here, boy." He was getting excited again.

"Woof, woof!" Jim was now the dog and then the helicopter appeared again.

Did they like playing with him, too?

Jim aimed an imaginary rifle at the helicopter. "Bang."

The helicopter left. Jim went to the side of the terrace. He looked down to the street. I don't know what he expected to see. He turned to me. The expression on his face was that of a small child. He looked into the sky. It was empty.

If there was a secret here, I didn't expose it. We never tore at each other's personas. We shared our philosophical baseball cards, just happy to be trading. We were counsellor to each other's camp. I never thought of survival in those days, I mean, my own getting on with life, raising a family, having kids, being a father. I only thought of being an artist. All of my activities were potential material for works of art. I felt close to Jim as I sensed his art activities were as important to him as mine were to me. The difference was that he made no effort to present them. It was up to me to open things up for discussion. Jim was concerned about other things, like would I give him a ride to the Lucky-U, this being the bar he liked to hang out at.

"I'm meeting Donna at four. Come along. It's a light thing."

The three of us sat in a booth. I remember this because it was the first time I'd ever sat down in the afternoon with two friends in a bar to drink beer.

"I'm not doing graduation," Jim announced out of the blue.

Jim never announced his moves. So he had something special to say.

"I only have brown shoes." Morrison offered gently.

We laughed.

"I found some grass I'd rather spend the dough on and a new edition of Rimbaud's poetry. He's my white shadow." Jim gave us a penetrating look, then added with a grin, "it's a better way to spend the afternoon."

"Who wants to become a penguin with a tassel?" I added.

We had a laugh and a sip of beer. It was fun sitting there away from campus. Away from our worlds in a neutral space we didn't have to be important. Jim and Donna got up to shoot some pool. The afternoon was young and I had my paintings waiting for me.

"Jim, if it's OK man, I'm going to my studio to paint." Making my statement declarative gave me the energy to split the scene.

"Fine man, Donna will take me home or I'll walk, no problem. Hey, go to it, man." His voice had the touch of a salute to it.

I had had a privileged childhood growing up in Rome, Italy, exploring the secrets of its history. At the end of the ruins, the monuments, the collections from past cultures, it is easy to understand that there is no point in war, in fighting to prove something. Hitting the other guy on the head is not going to knock any sense into it. Maybe there are exceptions like Hitler, when you can't step out of the way of megalomania. Perhaps if everybody were to have a privileged childhood they would see just how barbaric war is. They would learn to trust that it was OK to have secrets, that it was OK, because they were learning how to become artists. That could be everybody's quest.

Rome had shown me a cheerful way of hitting people over the head. On Christmas Eve it is the custom for people to gather at Piazza Navona with their friends. The plaza is filled with glass birds, angels, bells, delicate decorations for the holiday tree, sculpted Nativities and real shepherds and candied taffy being pulled and cut into small pieces and everybody brings a small broom with them.

In a gentle manner you are expected to tap the heads of your friends to remind them that they are to be more considerate of your feelings. This was the feeling I wanted in my work. In the Borghese Park, watching the Punch and Judy puppets, all the children knew that no matter how many times Punch hit Judy in the end, they would kiss and make up, promising not to hit one another again.

Our attention could then focus on the balloon that was escaping through the pine trees to enjoy its own freedom. In 1953 Rome was a happy city for me. Italian boys played soccer in the churchyard and I re-enacted movies with my friends. We understood about girls and how babies came into the world and I thought all that snickering was nasty. In my pre-pubescent purity I understood love and that Cyrano de Bergerac was very noble to try to get the girl for the handsome guy. David Brice and I were both in love with Elizabeth Trohill. Elizabeth seemed more interested in David, so I helped him with his relationship à la Cyrano de Bergerac, hoping secretly that I'd win out somehow in the end as Cyrano had. Our conversations concerning just how this should be achieved extended into a trip with his mom to Naples. We stayed over at a hotel and David and I got into a pillow fight. One of the pillows accidentally went flying out the window. Those pillows we threw out the window, wanting worlds by our side... a poetic moment of flight. When David's mother entered our room to investigate she found two boys laughing their heads off. This was about as far as we had gotten with solving his affair with Elizabeth. It did however inspire a few lines of poetry, which I wrote when I got back to Rome. The poem was modestly called I'M GREAT AND YET UNKNOWN.

I'M GREAT AND YET UNKNOWN

I'm great and yet unknown,
I act to conceal my reality,
Fearing that someone may think
If I take off my mask of dramatics…
I'm acting.
And so I'm bound to die unknown for my real
Greatness.
But before I do,
I'll state, I'm great.

This poem went on to achieve epic proportions but unfortunately I lost Elizabeth to David anyway. Perhaps it had something to do with the fact that I never sent her my poem… details, ol' boy, details.

We saw Brando in *Guys and Dolls* and heard Elvis on the terrace at Elizabeth's house. Playing spin the bottle we tasted the icky sweetness of a stolen kiss and understood that something lay ahead of us to know, some action that we would learn to do when we grew up. We knew that boys had this penis thing and that girls had something else and that we were supposed to join. What that felt like exactly, or how to do it was something none of us dare yet imagine. My first sexual encounter was totally unsolicited. Looking through the glass eye of our front door I saw that our maid had lifted her skirt and pointing to her panties she implored me to open the door: she wanted to show me what it was that boys do. Her urgency in this matter frightened me, even though I was safe behind the door. I went berserk and shouted at her that she should leave. When my parents returned I continued my antics, pacing on my bed. I insisted that they fire the maid. My parents, alarmed at my behaviour, took me to a psychiatrist, who never discovered the truth nor did he think it important. We had a good time playing cards and my parents were reassured that I was OK. Why had this so frightened me? The isolated moment, was it too strong? It was all right to have secrets. So if Jim wanted to howl at the helicopters, it was fine with me.

I had finished a large ink drawing four foot square on paper of a detailed skeleton flying spread-eagle over a city of endless buildings that had no windows, no signs of life. My skeleton seemed rather pleased with himself. He appeared to be dancing a wild jig. It was funny to look at, though I wasn't sure what I was trying to say. As I was pinning it up on my easel wall, I heard footsteps outside. My concentration would be broken, but I was happy that Jim was stopping by; he was the perfect audience for this drawing.

At the door Morrison doffed a naval captain's hat. I loved hats and went to see if it would fit me.

"Hey man, watch it, it's my dad's," Jim warned. I knew that he wasn't that possessive; it was just his way of showing respect. I placed the hat gently on my head.

"Come on in, buddy, show you what I've been doing."

Jim was carrying a paper bag. "Hey, the hat looks better on you. I'm putting a few beers in the fridge, OK? Want one?"

"Sure." We pulled the lids and sat down.

"You know Mike, I'd really like you to give me a drawing lesson. I'm impressed with the way that you suggest things rather than just put them down exactly," Jim observed as he took a seat. I tossed Jim a black fedora that I had stolen from my father's closet and he put it on. It looked funny on him and I began to laugh. It was the only time that I have seen Jim look ridiculous. He tilted it back in the style of one of the Bowery Boys and looked at himself in the kitchen mirror that was directly behind where he had been sitting.

"It looks fine like this…" he announced. "Let's see what happens if we wear them a while. Maybe we'll change fathers, too." It was a strange remark, and I didn't think that it would change us. I made no comment: it felt kinda funny as an idea.

"So you want a lesson in drawing, yeah?"

"Yeah, man, let me watch you work."

"Gee, Jim, that's kind of hard, ya know. It changes the vibes. But how about us doing a drawing together?"

"Great, man. Just what I was hoping you'd suggest."

I took out paper from my portfolio and cleared an area for work.

"Why don't we do elements of our dreams and see if they can relate somehow. We'll exchange at a certain moment and alter the images so that we are forced to expand our own concepts."

"Wow, Jim, that's great!"

"Yeah, that's what I was thinking. I mean, why not really divide the authorship of an image? It will come from both of us that way it might seem to be born of its own impetus."

"Heavy."

"Light."

"All right."

We were at it, chuckling like two kids in a sandbox. I put down a few marks with a bamboo pen.

"Why that?" Jim asked. "I mean, the line is so broad and irregular... Yeah, now I see what you're doing. Wait. Let me add something now." Jim bent down and very slowly and carefully drew a sort of Gorgon head, a mythic monster on top of an area where a face had begun to appear. I watched and felt the intensity and care that he was giving to our experiment. When he was done he looked at his work and then at me.

"What do ya think he wants for dinner?"

"I guess what all monsters want: pussy."

"Gee, Mike, I didn't know that you were capable of being as vulgar as me."

We chuckled.

"I said that for your benefit, Mr Morrison, guy."

"OK, I think we are getting the plan."

"What plan?" I inquired.

"Pussy, man. Lovely, sweet, young, clean, wet pussy."

We had finished our first beers and I offered to get us both another.

"Yeah. Pussy. I don't seem to see what I like. I mean, if I like them, I can't seem to fuck them. And if I fuck them, I can't seem to like them. What's my problem, Jim?"

"Did you ever go after someone that you really had the hots for?"

"I was rejected."

"Each and every time, Mike?"

"No."

"So?"

"I don't know. I want to make it as an artist, and, well, women want you to make money."

"Bullshit, Mike. Not someone who deeply digs you. Come on, man, you're just chicken."

I knew there was some truth to what Jim had spoken. I was chicken.

"Fuck it, Mike. One day your prick will be so hard and long you will be bound to score in spite of being a pimple-puss."

"You fucker," I said as I knocked my father's hat off of Jim's head. He did the same to me. The hats looked at us, waiting for our next move.

I took out my penis and began to empty my bladder out into the black fedora.

Jim took the challenge and filled his dad's hat as well. As we peed we whistled an old grade school hymn. The words were maybe different but the tune remained the same.

"Hitler was a jerk. Mussolini cut his weenie, now it doesn't work."

We were two characters out of Truffaut's *400 Blows*. We weren't stealing typewriters, we were claiming our territories like two dogs free to baptize the poles that had held each of us under control, called to order, held us in line. Fuck 'em! Piss on them! What the fuck were they doing for us now, now that we had grown too big for their laps? We were happy to wet down their authority and their laws. We were whistling Dixie now.

"Listen, Mike, why don't we put these pissoires out to air?"

"Yeah, let's leave the souvenirs on the boardwalk."

We chuckled like two gleeful pirates as we waved goodbye to the wet shapes that faced one another on the empty pavement.

Halfway back to my apartment we began to punch each other in a friendly way.

"Listen, dad," Jim said to me, "I've got to do some homework. Hold the drawing for me and I'll work on it with you later, OK?"

"Sure enough, dad. I can piss on it alone."

Some weight lifted as Jim disappeared up Thornton Avenue and I climbed the stairs to my pad. I felt elated, but also ambivalent; I knew that we both loved our fathers in spite of our anger, in spite of their blindness and fear of our youth. I wondered what it was like, growing up for Jim, his dad being an admiral. If sex represented some form of intimidation to me, I felt sure that the power of a huge naval vessel with its phallic guns and guys running around would be overwhelming. One and one may not be two; Jim could have had something altogether different on his mind, other than making fun of the authority of a police helicopter. Maybe he was just goofing, looking for what to do after graduation. Neither of us wanted to go to

Vietnam. Maybe we weren't afraid to die, we were afraid to kill. We could not be taught to hate. We had too much poetry under our belts. To kill was not a way to solve a problem. We wanted to jump to three, find a new solution. Maybe it was just about putting the focus on something else.

When Kennedy was shot everyone got glued to TV. It seemed that for hours the news repeated the tragedy in a state of disbelief, like a face washing itself over and over, unable to clean away the images of a horrible moment. A fact, a bullet, a terrible loss. It was real. It was not a game. They weren't children. I could not face TV. I went to the sculpture lab where I had been doing a head of Dylan Thomas. Without joy I filled this sad moment by building a series of columns in wet plaster. It was impossible to contemplate why this had happened. I was just busying myself. The forms I created reminded me of a phallus that my mother had taken from an Etruscan tomb; a marker designating that the person inside is male. Later she returned it, by giving it to our friend Prince Massimo, which was like giving it back to Italy. (As Prince Massimo was permitted to own and excavate antiquities, because his family origins reached back to the Empire days, my mother gave Massimo the phallic symbol she had taken, thinking it was sweeter and more easily accomplished than turning it in to the archeological authorities.)

I, too, was burying my President. I wanted him to enjoy the pagan pleasures of an Etruscan tomb. There he could listen to the flute players and watch the dancers as we lamented the passing of our Periclean Age. What eloquent style Kennedy had had! Picking up the dropped medallion, he had commented to the astronaut, 'from the Earth to the men of the sky'. Like Caesar stumbling on the sands of what is now Turkey, Kennedy had come, had seen and he had conquered our hearts. It was a question of style and intelligence. Kennedy had that effect upon me. I felt this intelligence. Even if it meant welcoming the Bomb.

At Bard College, in New York State, we all thought that the Cuban Missile Crisis was signalling the end of the world. This meant that we had to do something that would fit our perceptions of life; a sort of goodbye gesture. We adorned costumes and dragged out a cannon and gave speeches to welcome the Bomb. It was a post-Brechtian opera that we put on with our own three pennies. We were doing the only sensible thing. We were opening our arms and hearts in welcome, which was the only way we could disarm the monster. There was no point in greeting it with fear; if we greeted it with love then it could not hurt us. It was the way to disarm the Bomb. That was our thinking during the 60s. That was my thinking and I feel it was Jim's. Not everyone thought that way yet. The love generation and flower power began to bloom later.

In a state of wild abandon I dropped a garbage can from the third floor of my dorm. This was conceivably the most idiotic and numbskull gesture that I have ever made. Fortunately, no one below was hurt. What had I been thinking? Was I asking the Fates if we were right, that no one would get hurt, hit by the garbage can? Of course, we were right! But useless to test, that is what Oscar Wilde meant when he said, 'art is useless'. Politics are power, not poesy. We did not know the outcome of Vietnam. But when all wars end it is always about clean up and damage done. This process never changes. We don't seem to get better at solving our needs. Time is money is war is three. Change it, re-arrange it! Drugs are not hugs! Terrible confusion, fear, paranoia, learned responses, monkeys in a tree, is this thee? Not the free flowing beauty of a Roman fountain. Even a tiny bird can express the essence of everything beautiful. I was sober, standing in a park in winter, bored by my own thoughts before being electrified by this most marvellous creature. He began with Mozart and, not repeating himself, slipped into Beethoven, sidestepped to Chopin, made his crescendo with Rachmaninoff and then cooled his energies with a few side bars of Erik Satie. This concert was extraordinary and, to my amazement, it continued with Duke Ellington, Mahler, Stravinsky and his impressions of Shakespeare's Sonnets, Dante, and a riff from Henry Miller's *Colossus of Maroussi*. It was the greatest musical experience of my life.

Accountably, a lucky miss! I had been lucky as a child at Ranger Camp. I didn't want to go that summer. I wanted to be William Tell's son in the movie that Errol Flynn was to make. I had met Mr Flynn in Rome. Dad, mom and I had gone to bid him welcome. His monkey seemed to have the run of his apartment so we were stuck in the hallway and didn't stay very long. Mr Flynn admired a pin I was wearing so I gave it to him. The directness of my gesture pleased him and we started talking. That is, I did most of the gabbing. I informed him that I was also a painter and that I felt Picasso had influenced my earlier works, but now I was on the road in my own world. I was doing a series of drawings based on the fountains of Rome. I thought that they were very sexual, you see, water spouting out everywhere. I was very philosophical at 10. Mr Flynn wondered if I would put down my brushes and do my acting for him. I could play his son. Nothing of course would have pleased me more. Instead, as it turned out, I was shipped off to Ranger Camp. But still I didn't give up hope. I fashioned a bow and arrow and set to practising my skills. I cornered one of my roommates who agreed to put the apple on his head. I would put in a good word and perhaps he, too, could have a part in the movie with the famous Mr Flynn. I took aim and fired. The thin twig pierced my buddy's head and we both stood fixed for a moment looking at the arrow sticking out of his head. Without saying anything I calmly removed the arrow, which hadn't done much damage, and apologized for the bad shot and we let it go at that.

Practicing for Errol
ML 02

If only the adult world would play out its needs so harmlessly.

If only life were just a Punch and Judy show. If only we could all escape: unscathed. If only we could go to Piazza Navona with a broom perhaps we could sweep all the anger away. If only they had missed Kennedy. If only it had been the thud of the garbage can landing rather than the precious sensibilities that splattered across what was supposed to have been a lovely ride.

I have seen my father shot, stabbed and gunned down a thousand and one times in the movies... the make-believe world happily lets him come home for dinner. Wouldn't it be miraculous if all of our problems could be solved by the movies?

My father has played in films since 1933. By 1951 he had made over 90 appearances including a few classics, *The Ox-bow Incident* and *Key Largo*, for example. His voice and face were well known and both had an authority and power that were respected. In 1941 he played a mute in the film, *The Shepherd of the Hills*, which starred John Wayne. It was a shame that the sensitivity he displayed there was never explored in other films. Mostly he played the tough guy. You see there was a factor I didn't understand about my life. But how does a parent explain to an eight year old boy a political reality? My father had testified in Washington in front of the House Of Un-American Activities Committee. The consequences of this would develop in the future. The McCarthy period was a psychological bomb which exploded over and over. After my father's ordeal in Washington, my parents went to Europe to get away from the atmosphere of suspicion, fear and what would later be referred to as the witch-hunt of the McCarthy period. Reality was not explained to me nor were my father's mood swings. This became a part of the puzzle of my childhood which would be altered and expanded by my growing up in Europe. This book is the nature of my story, my aloneness... a single note in a sea of much larger troubles. This book is not a welcomed reminder and without Jim's help, I might be lost. My poetic posturing, my attitude of being the artist plus the political stigmata, are enough to signal some folks to keep moving. I'm not an approved rest station, a guy you can rave about that you've met on the 'in' list. Some accolades I am handed are short-lived. However I feel my position in society gives me an understanding of the harsh realities hidden from view... prejudice and ignorance of various kinds which are more subtly manipulated.

My art is in the nature of a diary. Essentially the actor has his own persona to work from. Josef von Sternberg complimented my father by saying that he had a cinematic mask that few people possess. This was quite true but what was also true is that he had the comic timing that even fewer actors are capable of. Woody Allen used a clip from *This Gun for Hire* in one of his films, which illustrates that kind of electric charge his work as an actor demonstrated. Actually if you look at his work as an actor from the point of view of watching a comic you better understand what he is doing. It is hard for me to say which of his films I admire the most. Probably *Key Largo*, even though it is only a cameo role. *The Asphalt Jungle* is probably his most definitive film work, but it brings an unpleasant memory. The actor is often confused with the actual person. In *The Asphalt Jungle* he is very convincing as a low life bookie who is the fall guy that confesses under pressure.

The District Attorney needs a pigeon to show he is halting illegal gambling and to appear as if he is cleaning up the city. My dad takes the rap. His character is also the person who sets up the deal between the thieves and a rich backer. The character who testified in Washington was just like the bookie in the film. This shadow would not leave my father. Even though he did get employment as an actor, he felt horribly guilty as a person for naming names. These realities stunted his career. When people refer to his performance in *The Asphalt Jungle* I wonder if they aren't also referring to his appearance in Washington, which was quoted widely in the newspapers and *Newsweek* magazine. My father hated himself for testifying, realising in retrospect that he had also created the wrong character for himself in Washington. The person I think he hurt the most was himself. The disfavour which would rub off upon my sister and myself created other inarticulated sentiments for my father as well. Under all the masks was the human being I knew my father to be; a man who is tender, gentle, sensitive and fragile like the character he played in *The Shepherd of the Hills*.

4

View From My Dashboard

Jim had no phone or car so I never knew when I'd see him. I imagine it was the same for everyone else. This added to the quality of surprise that Jim was building. His quiet intensity was a studied stance that I feel he had been working on a long time, the most recent nuances borrowed from Mailer's hero in *Deer Park*. Mailer talked to Jim about being on the edge, being finely tuned, being aware, ready to go, a western samurai, alert but relaxed. Having a car gave me mobility. I dropped in on Jim one evening. He said he had some acid, we could drop it together. There was also someone else there I sensed, his girlfriend at the time, I'm not sure. Anyway, we dropped it and separated into different rooms to get ready for the trip. It hit fast and seemed to go right through me. I was lying on the floor. It felt like my breath and heart had stopped and I was floating in a void. This passed and the trip seemed over. I got up and decided to go to my studio feeling wide awake and ready to do some work. I popped in on Jim who waved goodbye and drove to my small studio on Santa Monica Boulevard at Formosa.

This had been a funny trip, I thought, no hallucinations, no real loss of time consciousness, no mellow return to reality along the soft road of re-entry. If it was acid it was a small amount laced with speed. My studio had been bequeathed to me by my friend Forrest, who had left UCLA and the Fine Art Department for Berkeley and Architecture. Forrest and I had bummed our way across the states and spent the better part of the summer of 1964 visiting galleries and making a tour of the World's fair and the Bronx zoo, drawing with our Sumi brushes the animals and pretty girls that we saw everywhere. It was a unique summer. We would ride into the Village for a beer after painting my Uncle Marty's apartment for pocket money. Even though it was a sweltering July we didn't mind the work. Marty was always a cheery fellow and Aunt Marion was happy to have us as houseguests even though it was a small apartment. We played chess and discussed questions of divinity and the existence of God. Marty didn't buy into the existence of God; he disapproved that 'God' had become an excuse for mortal men to live irresponsibly. He went on to state that it was man's responsibility to create a morality that would be binding for people. He calmly explained the creation of 'God': finding it too painful for man to face reality alone, he created 'God' to keep him company and to pass on some of the responsibility of his actions to a force greater than his own. 'Heaven' and 'Hell', he continued, are states of being right here on earth.

The day that we painted Marty's apartment, I remember him turning around to look at Forrest and myself squarely. He put a hand to his lips, his balding head with its fine white hairs added something Zen Masterish to his handsome Mongolian features. He drew a smile and said, "Is there a God? Is there a flower? It is the same question... of course! And what is even more marvellous and fascinating to me is that it took billions of years to make a rose. To create a human mind out of what, hydrogen and carbon? What was the original element? Desire? It would seem that nature is self-sustaining. If we call that singularity 'God', does it mean that we also expect it to look after us? And we can hardly congratulate ourselves for just looking, but that is the wonder of it, that we get such pleasure in seeing. I feel that God would want us also to look after His garden and do marvellous things in it." Having said his piece, Marty ran off to take care of an errand, leaving me with a feeling of great enthusiasm. I felt both satisfied and excited; I might have even applauded. Forrest was also impressed.

Yes, it was an inspiring summer filled with the 'Pop' imagery of Wesselman, Red Grooms, Larry Rivers and a visit to Paul von Ringelheim's studio. Sitting on the stoop in front of Marty's apartment we talked with the janitor who was well versed in literature and we tried to make it with the girls down in the Village.

Forrest's studio had now become my private hideaway where I translated my hallucinations into etchings and large drawings.

Smoking grass aligned my thinking with the Surrealists' notion of automatic writing. I used my drugs for inspiration. I saw myself in the tradition of 'bad' boys like Baudelaire. (I had bought an expensive edition of his *Fleurs du Mal*, illustrated by one of my favourite sculptors, Sir Jacob Epstein. When I was fifteen I thought he was closer to the heart of capturing the soul of the sitter than Rodin. At that time Epstein and Degas were my heroes.) In my studio the work was moving in many directions. I was working on a large portrait of my father as a Forties gangster, the image he had been typecast in. I wanted a large, menacing face with a hat pulled down over one ear. I was also doing a series of paintings of my car, the chariot that took me from the LSD beach into the night and the glitter of neon in darkness, like jewels in a treasure chest.

One of my car paintings, a rather large one, caught my attention that night after dropping the acid at Jim's. It was a view of my dashboard with my hands on the wheel driving into a bucolic California landscape; the coast going up to Big Sur where green rolling hills and scrub oak trees twisted dramatically. I remember beginning with the sky. It bothered me; too flat. Picking up the brushes I worked furiously through the night, caught up in a new rhythm and facility I had not experienced before. The landscape nagged at me and I attacked it, as if pressed to repaint the entire history of landscape painting in one night, from Giotto to Cezanne and beyond. I kept scraping off the paint, stopping again and again, then I added a daub or two to the dashboard, which was going well. My two hands on the wheel driving into what? That was the point, what in the world was I trying to say? Was I going for a Sunday drive? Could it be a metaphorical ride? Where was I going? I worked like a madman pushed further and further into the paint, intoxicated by the smell of the turpentine. I was lost in the folds of paint deftly brushed into the ground of the canvas, wiped clean yet another time, scrubbed down to the tooth back for yet another beginning. Finally the paint took over. I had built a landscape of Boschian destruction, rivulets of muddy colour exploding in the distance.

Dawn came and I put down the brushes, exhausted and unable to see any further into the paint. I washed up and left the studio for a walk in the morning air, afraid that if I stayed at the studio I'd wind up scraping down the canvas once again. I had enough sense to walk away from it to let the painting sit in peace for a while, let everything settle. Later I could make a judgement with a fresh eye. Having a coffee and doughnut at Winchell's, I looked at the morning people. They were so blissfully unaware of my night wrestling with paint, with art history, with my soul. I realised I lived outside, away from their mundane realities. Their weekend lay before them. I felt that I had just used mine up in one long gulp. I walked back to the studio and crashed.

The bed was in a dark alcove. I pulled the brown blanket up to my chin, the warm sweet odour that lived in that room felt good. I closed my eyes and fell into a deep void. Asleep, I was greeted by a vivid dream. I was in a silent world. The sky was bright like the collages back on Jim's wall. There was a beautiful woman ahead of me beckoning. The moon and the stars were out even though it was daytime. I sat down at a table and Jim came over. He was dressed in black and looked cleaner and handsomer than I had remembered him. He motioned to me. I got up and saw I was at the seaside. Waves were crashing against deeply chiselled cliffs bristling in the sunlight. I turned. There was no one to be seen. I felt as if I were the only person now left in the world, but I felt very full, complete. The hills rolled on toward the horizon, a sweet wind in the air.

I awoke late in the afternoon, unsure of where I was exactly. I seemed to be full of energy and jumped out of bed. I sauntered into the studio forgetting that I had painted anything the previous night. God, what a mess! I was almost startled to see it. What a lovely convincing mess! It looked like I was driving into the end of the world. Then I thought, *yeah, this painting is for Jim*. He didn't judge me the way people judged my father. I wanted Jim to have it; I felt he had given me a friendship. It was his openness and the sense of pleasure I had being in his company. I didn't feel that way with most people. It was his intelligence which I found appealing. It was there like a glass of water. A mischievous joy accompanied the task of tying my wet painting to the back of my TR3 Triumph. I'd sneak it down Santa Monica Blvd. to Jim's apartment. I was nervous about his reaction and was relieved that he wasn't home. I left the painting as a surprise. Neither of us had phones so it would come up at a chance meeting.

At that time he never mentioned it and I never asked. I thought that perhaps he'd given it away or maybe someone had stolen it. My hands on the wheel of the car, driving into the apocalypse, into chaos. My canvas born of a night we had begun together was now free to have its own life, just like the aspiration of some of Jim's songs were ours.

In the beginning of *The End*, his apocalyptic lyrics seem to refer to my Roman childhood and my parental problems. The climactic moment was his dialogue with his father and mother whom he ritually kills and makes love to like Oedipus. This song was the primal experience of the 60s, which few could face even though the story is a Greek classic. It was pulled from his consciousness and laid naked one night at the Whisky à Go Go. From that moment on their politics were clear. The Doors and Jim were not an entertainment, but a part of the theatre of revolution.

5

Clay Portraits And Judy Garland

At that time I used to go to Barney's and write in this lovely notebook. This pastime always made me think of the child in *400 Blows* now grown up to write his memoirs in English at Barney's sipping Irish coffees and feeling like Shakespeare, very grand and a tad above it all. I didn't go to Barney's so frequently. But one afternoon I sat and wrote as I consumed five Irish coffees. That notebook was later discovered by an aunt, who was so upset with the 'dirty words' I had used that she threw the book away. It's too bad as I'd be curious to know what thoughts I had then and where I imagined I was going. It was in that notebook that I had a souvenir photo of Jim and me. I was reading Tennessee Williams' short stories, which I had bought at City Lights Bookstore during a

Christmas trip I had made with Sandra whom I adored. I desperately wanted to make love with her but she was unsure. I think she wanted me to get to work with the artists she introduced me to in San Francisco. I was seventeen then and didn't understand her need or the stories I was reading. So my experience became something to write about. Riding the Greyhound into the grey and cold of San Francisco, meeting older artists struggling to find the time to do their own work, getting paid by the hour in gloomy studios for other artists, wasn't so romantic when Sandra wasn't encouraging me. The ride back to LA at Christmas Eve on the Greyhound alone with an assortment of silent people huddled against cold glass windows was as shabby as a story by Williams without alcohol or sex. The bus stopped once to let a single person descend into the night. I had been watching him drink from a paper bag. When I walked into my parents' living room that night a small party was going on and I was not made to feel welcome. They were into their own world so I went to my room and tried to read more Williams. Moving from one place to another, what I took with me was how I'd build a new life. Going to Rome it was a pirate's pistol... returning to America it was a desire to make art. That is what people did who didn't quite fit in. I examined my past in my notebooks.

   My parents took me to a cocktail party in Beverly Hills at the home of a plastic surgeon. Their daughter was attending Beverly Hills High where I'd be going the following semester. Carol was elusive so I fell into conversation with a painter, Mark Cheka. (Years later Mark and I worked together on a large mural, played ping pong and developed an intimate art movement called Meow-purr). At the cocktail party I asked him where I could get lessons in sculpture. Vito had a subterranean studio under Gold's Gym on Beverly Blvd. I could bus it. I was fifteen and he had nude models and he called the housewives who attended his evening classes 'bunnies'. I was his youngest pupil and an eighty year old Russian lady was his oldest client; she was a 'bunny' as well. It was a thrill to be working from live models and Vito, sporting a Fu Manchu moustache, bounced about with enthusiasm and gusto. There was a focus in his class, which made sense, we all wanted to learn. We enjoyed developing our skills. There was a purpose in what we were doing.

Much less enjoyable were my high school classes. Of these, my English courses were the most tolerable. Stanton Kaye, a classmate, told me he had an idea for a play about a man who was completely blind, but once a year his vision would return for three minutes. It was these precious moments that he lived to see. The set would be old shoes hanging from the ceiling. Stan had discovered a group of poets living in San Francisco, 'the beats'. He'd been up there and was proud of the sandals he wore. Stan was looking for passion elsewhere, too.

One summer I got a commission to do a large garden sculpture for a backyard overlooking a pool of a modern house designed by Rex Lotery, the architect. I had completed a sculpture in high school where we worked from a mixture of cement, plaster and Zonolite. I poured a block three and a half feet high in my backyard and set to work each morning banging away with a wood chisel and a hammer, to make my 'Adam and Eve'. It was a passionate activity; the sound of my working disturbed the neighbours so I had to wait until nine o'clock to begin my hammering. Within a month I completed my commission and saw it installed. Everyone was pleased, but I was surprised no other architectural commissions materialised from this project, even though I was merely eighteen.

Most occurrences in high school seemed to evaporate. I presented my clay portraits in a small showcase in the hallway but few students made any comments. I participated in school plays but my father never attended. Eddy Robinson Jr. came over to our apartment one afternoon and began to cry seeing the heads I had been doing, which included a monumental terracotta of my father. I read young Robinson's autobiography. He too had wanted to be an actor but he didn't have his dad's toughness. He was tall and sensitive-looking, a gentle man who would one day commit suicide.

I was accepted as a special student at Otis Art Institute. The painter, Fletcher Martin, a picturesque soft spoken man with a large handlebar moustache, told me that in painting, light and dark follow each other to carve out space. He sent me off to Otis, where he taught, to learn more. It was thrilling to work alongside older painters as we were all interpreting the same subject. A series of doors sat mysteriously in front of us, their weather-beaten facades suggesting that they could tell stories of all the people who had opened them and passed through them to enter into the moments of their lives… now faded echoes. I explored a world of greys, warm red greys and cool blue tones. The world of memory and shadow was also being uncovered by the movies that were made of Tennessee Williams' plays. Williams' language had a soft sound, the meanings went deep. My doors were like a theatre set, perhaps our professor also admired Williams.

My life in high school was in itself a series of small theatrical vignettes. The making of clay portraits gave me the most satisfaction and received the most attention. Richard Basehart, the actor, had a very beautiful face and George Tobias, a character actor, had a curious expression, almost an absent-minded quality. They were both close friends of my parents and I had known George since I was a child of five. Making their portraits had this special connection in time. They were both excellent models and the results were pleasing, a rough freshness which caught their character. Basehart wanted to know why I'd want to sell him his head, didn't I want it? Today I'm sorry I didn't keep it. I think Mr Basehart had a kind of wisdom. I saw him in a production of Shakespeare's Henry V; he was as fine an actor as any I've ever watched on stage. My father rushed in to see how my portrait was developing of George Tobias. He accidentally knocked the head over and my efforts to re-establish what I had achieved never equalled what I had caught. George never forgave my dad; the existing head is not as dramatic. This portrait I inherited from George after he passed on.

I did eventually get several commissions to make my heads into bronze. The foundry I chose was in Venice. Alf Peterson did everything himself. It was a veritable junkyard but fine artists also cast their works there. Rico Lebrun's wax torsos were like suits of armour, handsome, ominous brown wax curves. And there was Charles Fraiser, who cast a globe with toys over it and helped with my first bronze casting. It was of my grandfather, Israel Goldsmith. He had sat for drawings and it was from these drawings that I had worked. When I was twelve I spent six months living with my grandfather. My grandmother had passed on and my stay with my grandfather was practical, both from the standpoint that I would offer him my company, and because I could continue my schooling in California. My stay with him was peaceful and orderly. Israel was gentle with me, closer in many ways than my own father. Everything changed after my father went to Washington. We were never really close. He avoided my affection. Once in a while I'd see his smile, hear his laughter. He was like a caged animal, I was afraid of him. He had to audition in real life to see if he'd be accepted, like a traveller who goes to a foreign land without knowing the language or customs, he had to interpret nuances not stated clearly or put too bluntly. Sometimes he was victimised by his own imagination. He didn't want me around. I remember in London he sent me out of the house once, I didn't have anyone to visit. Still, he was correct not to subject me to his rage. My grandfather could afford to be pleasant. We played cards (mostly poker) and went to the drive-in movies every Thursday. Our closeness then was an element that I wanted to work into my portrait of him; his tenderness and dignity. I remember that once I broke a window. I thought that my grandfather would be angry with me. "Be more careful next time," he advised with a smile.

La Cienega Blvd. was then the centre of the art world in LA. On Monday nights people flocked to the galleries, a social stroll. One evening there were silver pillows floating in a gallery. It was a delightful vision but I couldn't accept this as art. It would be much later that my appreciation of Andy Warhol's point of view would be cherished. The 60s had broken; we read Playboy and our President was young. There was a fresh powerful focus to being alive. Living around the Sunset Strip area I was able to walk to the coffee houses and it was easy to meet and get to know various celebrities. Comedians like Harvey Korman and Professor Irwin Corey (you can get more with a kind word and a gun) often came to Puppi's bistro for coffee and their house pastries. Andre Philippe, an actor/singer was a catalyst; his gregarious and cheerful nature brought people together. One afternoon he took me with him to meet and draw Judy

Garland, whom he was seeing socially.

Walking down the hall of CBS we passed the tall and menacing actor Richard Boone 'Paladin' on the way to Judy's dressing room. It was not the best moment to be making a drawing of Ms Garland who was extremely nervous about her TV comeback. She was hardly aware of my presence. Barbra Streisand was to debut that night. I drew both of them.

Their performances were each lovely but I never developed the drawings into anything to present to them. I wasn't that professional then. I didn't fully appreciate how special or privileged that moment had been. It was a fluid period; there would be time enough to get serious. It was Andre who gave me my first vial of LSD. He had scored it from Timothy Leary. It was legal then, seen as an extension of how we were all moving forward to embrace yoga, Zen, vegetables, fresh air, grass, music, meditation, art, poetry and the newest elixir for freedom, LSD.

6

Salvador Dalí At The Seaside

In 1964 Venice, California was desolate during the winter. My choices during that grey season were either working directly in the mornings, or a pleasant escape; the walk a block away to the long flat bay of sand. The studio *en plein air*. I had this landscape all to myself and it was good to go away from the soft presence of the electric crackle of my shantytown out into the vast open wetness of the salt air. Back in my studio kitchen I'd melt wax and pour the brown liquid onto tinfoil before mushing shapes into it. The room soon became a changing collage of unfinished projects but their expectant nature appealed to me. They beckoned to me, holding a trail of my own thoughts in ransom. One figure I recall was of a Buddha sitting on a wagon. The figure in wax had a texture to suggest antiquity; the deterioration made by time. Another wax was an abstract shape. Mostly I remember the horrible linoleum floor, which I eventually tore up.

It was raining cats and dogs. There was a knock at the door.

"This is Dwayne. He needs a place to stay."

Morrison dashed out and I had a new roommate for a couple of weeks. Dwayne was from Kansas; his idea of art was to collect road signs, 'Dead End'. He was a lost fellow. We shared our peanut butter sandwiches and I tried to explain to him what a Jew was. It amazed me how many young people from the Midwest expected us to have small horns hidden under our coiffures. I think Jim was giving me a lesson on where I was, what America was about outside the pages of Norman Mailer or Aldous Huxley. I was reading Huxley's *The Doors of Perception*, a title suggested by William Blake's writings:

'If the doors of perception were cleansed, everything would appear

to man as it truly is, infinite'.

I had toothpaste in my mouth one winter morning when Jim came in without knocking.

"You didn't wait for me," I accused.

"I did. I was there one hour. One whole fucking hour," Jim responded harshly.

"Jim," rinsing the toothpaste out of my mouth, "you're a fucking liar. You went to Felix's. What did you get?"

"How do you know I went to Felix's?"

"Because I waited and you didn't show."

"Oh," Jim's face relaxed into a smile. "Got any orange juice?" Now he was full of grins.

"Yeah." I was getting the idea. Jim had scored elsewhere.

He removed two vials of aqua-blue acid. I poured out two small glasses of OJ.

"Twinkle, twinkle," he said, emptying the vials.

It was a block and a half stroll to the boardwalk. In spite of the fact that it was a beautiful day, we had the beach to ourselves. We took our shoes off and walked across the sand to be near the place where the water touches the shore. The waves were gently lapping and we were in a good mood.

Sitting on the isolated beach waiting for the trip to come on, the ocean seemed to be winking at me. A troupe of sandpipers appeared, running like electric bumper cars which also stop seemingly without warning. Their activity was precise and funny. In fact, everything was uproariously funny. Jim touched my shoulder and pointed to the shoreline. There was Salvador Dalí lifting up the ocean like a slice of roast beef. He materialized quite naturally from the thin cerulean sky so familiar in his early paintings. I was not surprised to see him; I was most flattered. He was there for an instant, not enough time to discuss his theory of 'critical paranoia', which is the hallucination of things inside of forms, the basis of his subconscious realism. His demonstration only lasted a moment before he moulded into the crepitating waves wearing dancing stars. He was in a hurry and I was left giggling.

The sea was filling up with boats, but they were not the boats from the Marina, they were boats from Phoenicia. We were watching them from the coast of Asia Minor... the shape of Jim's foot was a dead giveaway. He was Alexander the Great. My mind was fluid with sensation, imitations of places with personalities. We watched the boats drifting by. Soon we would take the whole world for a lovely holiday, take them away from their schedules, their prejudices, their fears, show them life as a celebration, a gathering of joyous spirits, of shared revelations, of pure love, of pure sex, of divine fecundation. As Rimbaud had dreamed, 'Christmas on Earth'.

That is the meaning of hallucination, hailing the world, stopping it dead in its tracks, shouting, 'Hallelujah... LIFE IS!' ...and that is all, that being rejoices in being, being for the sake of being. Because it is being that is what is. Because being is reality unto itself. Not reflecting, judging, evaluating, composing, just being... bang... SATORI... I am that I am.

And sitting on the crystalline jewel box, pushing the grains of sand around in the ever clear light, breathing in the physically present presence of the soothing airy glue that fills the lungs, the thought of dying didn't seem like a terrible fate. Where else would one go, where else was there but the present presence of all things around one? Forms changed, rocks gave way to soil, but it was all here, it had always been all here and always would be all here. For a moment I had lost or given up my own little cabin of reality and become a part of the infinite. The infinite doesn't look at itself. It rolls on as one absolute entity in a flux of time-space, holding elements and thought all in all. It doesn't make a living at or on anything, it just is.

I felt chilled. Where was I? I found myself perched on a rock on the shoreline, fingers clenching and unclenching the grit of grains of sand. They were cold. I was cold. Where did this fog come from? My God, where was Jim? I was totally alone. I had no one to talk to. I got up and began to walk away from the sound of the waves and into the darkness, thinking, 'we have all left the Kingdom of Heaven and gone looking for a job'.

7

Descending The Staircase With Duchamp And Jean Harlow

It is quiet in Venice sitting at my coffee table. I can see the ocean, just an inch or two of it between the houses. It's more steely grey than the grey that was the winter of my senior year at UCLA. Gary Gagh moved in with me. (Later he would move to San Francisco where he developed into a fine poet. He had beautiful almond shaped eyes and told me he had read my mother's radio plays.) We were each paying thirty-two fifty for this two-bedroom flat on the second storey. It was a walk-up apartment in the front facing Thornton Avenue. Gary flipped on a trip. I felt responsible. I had said that I would look after him, but I got distracted watching Tom dance on the beach for a group of Asians who were amused by his parading. Gary had disappeared and I learned later that he had gotten into some kind of paranoid state and had starting imitating a dog. This had happened in the corner grocery store and must have scared the elderly Jewish proprietor who had called the police. When they came he apparently bit one of the cops on the leg. I didn't find out about this for some time. I thought it was very funny, an absurdist vignette, but I also felt sorry for him. I'm sorry man! He moved out and I spent several weeks alone working on various projects. Days passed listening to The Rolling Stones while I painted and worked on my notebook building stories that I hoped to eventually resolve into a novel. By this time I was a seasoned eccentric. I wasn't going out much, I had withdrawn into a kind of cocoon.

It was easy however for me to become distracted from my own work. The Beatles sang of love and we all went crazy over *A Hard Day's Night*. It was the first breath of mass media joy since Kennedy's assassination. I went to see the film with my friend John. (John S. Bragin and I were friends from high school. We had gone to Bard College together where he presented a film course as an entertainment. It was John who introduced me to Jim Morrison at UCLA.) John and I queued up outside with a group of young girls in the Pacific Palisades. Although they were twelve and thirteen years old, they wanted to give the impression of being much older. They looked like thirty-five-year-old midgets, chatting away, very fashionable, talking clothing and style. It amused us. They weren't out of high school yet; we would be graduating from college. One would have confused our ages judging from the conversations.

My college friends and I were searching to make our own visions, hard pressed by Vietnam, in a world that seemed indifferent, assured of its right to continue on a course that seemed like pure madness. Madness, war, society as a herd instinct, it is all a form of death penalty. The death penalty is not merely the result of actually putting someone to death. We also condemn the living by our own interpretations of what we feel they deserve, based on how we think they behave. Social discrimination. A remark said in passing, a death sentence. I had heard remarks about my father, they hadn't realised I was his son. Vietnam sat on us. It weighed me down. I was so serious in 1963. I'd hear of some event and drive out to meet it hoping for some breakthrough.

I went early to see the Marcel Duchamp Retrospective in Pasadena. I was the first one there. I walked into a room where there was a chess set sitting on a table with two chairs. There was nothing else in the room. Momentarily Duchamp walked in, also alone. The glance I received from Duchamp told all, 'the struggle any artist has lasts a whole lifetime'. Cubes of marble the size of sugar cubes filled a birdcage, a shovel leaning up against the wall felt curious, delightful. Dada art was a way to break through conventional ideas, the visual humour often dressed elegantly. Using materials not usually associated with art had a shock value. It was a cubist painting that first put Marcel in the spotlight: *Nude Descending the Staircase No. 2,* his entry for the 1913 Armory Exhibition in New York City. I left the exhibition early and went to see a young girl whose paintings I admired, but she wasn't in. Later I learned that she had driven to a gas station and poured gas over herself and lit her body. This demonstration never made the papers. We revere the saints as we watch them burn. Jim Morrison wanted to be Hamlet, Jesus, Mohammed, Buddha, all wrapped into one package, one evolution of a soul, or maybe it was my unconscious wish. Isn't that the notion of evolution? A chance to be naked, that is all we have. A chance to reach out and, like children, see the world as it truly is, freshly created each day. It is we who persist, unable to play and greet each encounter with wonderment, making up something new. We use the same roads over and over, say the same things: we bore ourselves, shield ourselves, we blind ourselves from the fun of thinking of new things to say, a different way to see the reality that is in front of us. How would Jesus greet you? How would Chaplin twirl his cane, interpret the moment? How would Michelangelo use the opportunity to see form? What could I say or do to wake up the moment? We didn't create a single flower but we did create Flower Power. Perhaps God is another word for beauty or Beauty another word for god. It is all how you see it and what you do with it. Creation.

   I had been up to San Francisco to meet Michael McClure. He impressed me as a very elegant man. He looked like a young Tyrone Power with long hair. I rode with him and Bruce Conner to hear recordings of his *Beast Language* poems, which he had recited to the lions at the zoo. It was a fateful way to salute the primordial, to cross over to the animal kingdom and reaffirm affinities lost long ago. I was lucky to be able to stay with Bobbie up in San Francisco. Roberta Hill was as subdued and gentle as the delicate plant on her coffee table, which seemed to shake in our presence somehow mirroring her fragility. Her apartment was a quiet environment where I devoured her collection of a poetry anthology called *Fuck You Magazine of the Arts.* It was a comprehensive, up-to-the-last-minute mimeographed series of all the best works, unavailable at City Lights Book Store. I discovered many poets and their music in between visits to McClure's apartment.

Michael told me he was very struck by the structure of John Webster's plays. We discussed his play *The Beard*, a sensual, sexual ego game of dominance between Billy the Kid and Jean Harlow. He asked if I would be interested in doing the play. I'm not sure what he meant at that time… acting, sets, et cetera. I was interested in poetry and in trying to write poems. I asked him if he had any special techniques for writing. Michael said that sometimes he would write down a hundred words, words that he felt were really close to him, and then he would build structures around them. The idea was so novel to me that I asked him if I could try it out right then and there. I sat on his living room floor and wrote out a list of words and then proceeded to write a poem. The technique seemed to work well for me and I left Michael's apartment in a state of poetic glow.

Michael McClure gave me a pack of his word cards. At each end of a card, a single word was printed. Moon, April, Woman, Glove, Knife, Glow, Veil, Soft, Dark, Press, Wine, Hiss, Grain, Beam, Space, Cry, Silk, Bread, Blue-Black, Edge… it was his 'Dream Table'. Fan the cards with your thumb and create word poems. Shuffle and reinvent. Marigold mantra Michael McClure.

Under Michael's spell I went to the zoo to test his beast language. As I approached the lions I bellowed "Grar, GhHarrar, Ghahoar", the tigers thought I was idiotic. Undaunted, I pressed on to the lions who were next door. Again I bellowed mightily "GRAAAHOAR". An old lion rolled over surrendering to my antics. I felt a bit of a bully, the other people around laughed. I felt sorry for the old lion.

Back in LA I did a painting for Michael… an icon presumably showing Billy the Kid's black boot. As a gesture in the mood of Billy, I printed under the boots: 'Mike, Kiss my Black Boots'. I thought McClure would get a kick out of this kind of bravura.

8

Peace Pipe

As the day got greyer, I became more subdued. The buildings outside offered some humour; they seemed to have been drawn by Paul Klee, linear and somehow amusing. I sat calmly looking out of the bay window letting the thoughts drift through my mind. I tried to evaluate why I had become an outsider. It was never my choice. The questions usually started with that memory of a curtain that my mother had painted. As a child I imagined things happening on it before dozing off to sleep, or looked beyond it, wondering when my parents would be returning. One day they said that they would see us in a 'couple of days'. We did not see them for a couple of months. My sister Toni, then three and-a-half, and I were left in the care of my dad's older brother Jack and his wife Elaine. They moved into our home on Fulton Avenue in the San Fernando Valley in LA. This was harder on my sister, who tried to conjure up her parents' attention long-distance by destroying my vegetable garden before I got up to water it, which I did religiously. We were young animals responding instinctively in a crisis we did not understand. One night my sister was locked outside the front door in an effort to put a stop to her crying. To stop her sobbing, I led Toni into my room where we played with my marbles. Soon Toni was smiling. She is like a dolphin, diving in and out of emotions, always living in the present, carrying no baggage from the past. Aunt Elaine's nature did not allow her to let us get physically close to her. She loved us as best she could, pouring egg malts down us as if we were recuperating from a long illness.

My first imitation of an actor was of my father. He is in a phone booth and talking quickly because he knows that he is about to be shot to death. I hadn't actually seen him performing this scene, I'd only heard about it. By the age of five I had perfected this take-off and it had gotten a big response from my parents' friends. Artie Auerbach especially enjoyed working out routines with me. This hub of activity was now over. I would now have to be the good soldier. A friend of my uncle's was a colonel and he gave me his cap, which reinforced my new job. I liked hats and the colonel liked me. I had just lost my favourite hat, a black Hopalong Cassidy hat that I especially cherished because I had spoken to Hoppy over the phone before my parents left us. He was my first TV hero. Someone had taken this hat right off my head while I was riding my bicycle around the block, an activity I no longer enjoyed.

I was always the good soldier, always saluting and standing at attention. Posing for photographs, I stood rigidly to show our parents who were now in Europe. I smiled like a demon trying to show them that it was hard… it was a hard smile. Toni, on the other hand, always managed to be photographed in the act of crying. She, too, knew who the photos were for. Four months later when we greeted my mother at the airport, I sang her one of her favourite songs, Rodgers & Hammerstein's *Dites Moi*, from South Pacific. Toni turned to address Aunt Elaine.

"You can go home now; I don't need you." My mother never forgot Toni's statement. I never realised how frightened she had been or how damaged her psyche would be by my parents' disappearance.

I laughed, letting off my own steam. I would not have to be the good soldier any longer. Elaine was deeply hurt; she had meant well.

A few days later, I asked my mother why the kids at school did not like me. We sat in the backyard. My mother passed around a cigarette, the peace pipe, and explained that we were descendants of the Iroquois tribe. Indians were not well liked. It was a good enough substitute for the moment. My father's presence in Washington to testify in front of the House Un-American Activities Committee changed the pleasant realities of my family life. My sister and I made our own adjustments. Most often political situations are clearly defined. In my sister's and my own case, this was not so. We would each discover and respond to different nuances of this ostracism or *black list*.

My father eventually wrote an autobiography to explain his own terrors, confusions, guilt and choices. He had told the truth in Washington but paid a high price personally, as everyone would be called to do caught in the web of the McCarthy period. Three months later we were sailing out of New York on the USS Constitution. I enjoyed this trip, singing Al Jolson songs for sundaes and exploring the big ship. I remember seeing the small figure of a man standing on the dock in Naples. I recognised dad from the hat he was wearing. We waved to each other as his figure grew larger. My father was to star in several Italian films, and Rome was to become a very special backyard. There were things Roman which told their own stories, taught their own lessons, and there were also things American to search out: peanut butter, pancakes and movies. It was the movies that recreated America.

As the light dwindled I felt alone, isolated. Wouldn't it be nice if Roberta came down from San Francisco and visited for a bit? I would write her and see. We had had such a good time in San Francisco going to parties, even our visit to Tom was kind of fun. He was obnoxious, but then, he had been on acid. Funny how Roberta knew she was going to win that cake, sitting there in the audience just waiting to pick up her door prize. I can't remember whether it was a play or a poetry reading that we were attending. It was lovely being with her in San Francisco, quiet and smooth in her presence. Would she come to see me? I needed something to look forward to. I lit a candle thinking to recreate our atmosphere and wrote her a poem, which I mailed.

9

Ten Year Old Antique

Survival, kid, wake up, you've got to get with it. What was I supposed to get with? All that may have made perfect sense at one time, I had lost the thread of. I'd pick it up again. I had my words, my paints, my clay and wax. I ate food, I took drugs and it was fun. And, yeah, sex. Sex. What had happened to that lust I had felt in high school, riding to school on the bus with a hard-on? God, I had three girlfriends at a time. I threw the best parties. Everyone wanted me to paint their portraits or make a sculpture of them, where were they all now? God, I even loved rubbing up against Sandra, coming in my pants behind her mother's car in the garage. She was so sensual, she smelled so good, her skin was so white and tight. I loved putting my tongue in her mouth, I couldn't get enough of it. Yeah, now sex seemed rather overwhelming, too rich. Maybe it was that time I took acid and walked into Ruth's bedroom; she looked ripe, oozy, I just couldn't go over to her bed. I became a frozen mannequin myself. It was a matter of not having it up and ready to go, couldn't break the ice. Maybe it was Ruth's pleading that drove me back into the hallway. That's why I liked Roberta; she was so quiet. I could be the aggressor, but then again, we never had taken acid for sex. I needed sex. It distracted me from this crippling sensitivity. It gave me sufficient strength, a sense of my animal self. Acid had broken down some of those fibres, fibres that were always a touch weak. Maybe that's why I had had so many girlfriends in high school; they felt secure in my company. I never gave the impression of being on the make. But I sure wanted it. I wasn't cool, I was just artistic, distant, moody, or I resorted to showing the girls my art work or doing my comic bits, my impersonations of Chaplin, Jacques Tati, Bogart. My bits were never corny, they had been pieced together over a long period of time. I met Humphrey Bogart when I was a kid in Rome and had made him laugh. I had style. Dad had taken me to meet Bogie. Apparently my father had told him about my running away from home. I hadn't been getting enough attention from my mother, who was busy writing, so I'd packed my bags and headed out, saying "I can't stand that woman".

   I had placed my hat collection on top of my head, one hat on top of another. The tower of hats included a fez, and a blue cavalier's chapeau with a red ribbon crest – my favourite because it had a feather like Cyrano's. I suspect it was the pronouncement, "I can't stand that woman," that piqued Mr Bogart's interest rather than the amusing figure I must have cut walking down the street before my dad offered me a ride to wherever I was going. Upon hearing this story, Bogart said that he wanted to meet me. It was before I knew who he was or that my father had made two films with him, *Key Largo* and one of those 'breaking out of jail' flicks, typical of the early Forties.

   Humphrey Bogart and Lauren Bacall were staying at the Excelsior Hotel. We met them in the posh bar just off the main lobby. After

introductions Bogie asked if I wanted to get an autographed picture of him. He thought that I was cute and was charmed by my calling him 'Home-free', my English having taken on an Italian accent. So off we went for the autograph. Mr Bogart asked if I minded if we walked up, explaining that he needed the exercise and it was only one flight up to his room. This was okay with me and I followed him up the richly carpeted circular flight that skirted the small glass elevator.

Mr Bogart didn't have to turn the light on in his room; there was enough light coming from the hallway to illuminate the drawers of his large shipper trunk, which he said he hadn't unpacked yet. My eyes followed his movements. Opening one drawer, I could see stacks of ten thousand lira bills. "Oops, wrong drawer…" The second one had the photo. "Oh, gee, it's the only one left… listen kid, it's an old one… ten years old, I hope you don't mind?" "No, Mr Bogart, that will be fine." "Humphrey, call me Humphrey." "Okay, Home-Free." Bogart delighted in my mispronouncing his name. During this interlude, Bogie had autographed the picture, "To Mike, Best wishes, Humphrey Bogart." On the way downstairs, I felt I should say something that would make him feel better about his parting with a photo that was ten years old and his last.

Downstairs, I blurted out, "Look, I've got an antique, it's ten years old, it's valuable."

Bogie enjoyed this and laughed openly. In creating an instant antique, in the ancient city of Rome, I had made a fan out of Mr Bogart.

Bogart and Bacall had to go somewhere, but 'Home-free' said that he would like to see me again; maybe papa would bring me by and I could spend a weekend with him during the summer on his boat. I never did see Bogart in person again. But I tried to see all his films, including the one that he was making when I met him. *Beat the Devil* is today an underground classic. At the time of its release it was a financial fiasco. After two weeks of filming, John Huston, who had put the project together and was directing, is reported to have said while watching the rushes, "well, boys, I think we had better make this one a comedy". It became one of my favourites and I used to delight the girls by re-creating the entire *mise en scène* of oddballs that Huston placed in this quirky adventure. Peter Lorre's little dialogue, written by a young Truman Capote, was a natural gem to imitate. In his typical whining voice, Lorre intones, "Time: the Swiss manufacture it, the Italians squander it, the French relish it, the Americans abuse it. Time, if you ask me, I think time, time is a thief."

10

Chaplin And Other Early Heroes

In Rome I saw Charles Chaplin in *Modern Times*. It was always the most personal touches that I took delight in trying to copy. It was the song that he makes up, in a non-existent language, that delighted me. It was like watching the children play in the school yard when I first came to Italy. Watching them and listening to them without understanding exactly what it was they were saying, I got the gist of what they meant. I enjoyed the film so thoroughly that I sat through it twice. It was great fun watching the sequence of events as Chaplin goes crazy, turning the bolts in the factory, and then turning the buttons on the dress of a bosomy lady while making his escape. The stringing together of visual metaphors was the signature of his genius. The button gag took Chaplin on his adventure. Europe became my inadvertent adventure. I loved the song he sang in *Modern Times* as a singing waiter. Losing the words, which were written on his cuffs, he made up a song in double-talk French and Italian, which is how I understood my world in Rome. His songs were all insightful. I would later discover, they were his philosophies!

"Live in the moment, make it up as you go along, life off the cuff, as it were."

In *The Great Dictator*, he impersonates Hitler and makes him ridiculous by having him play with a balloon globe, lightly tapping it into the air, and then playing football with it, showing us how childish megalomania is. Chaplin was funny and profound at the same time.

At that time in Rome there were only two movie houses that showed films in English aside from the Embassy Theatre, which was called the 'Maag'. All week long I would try to wangle a ticket out of one of my school chums, who were privileged because their parents were connected to the American Embassy or to the Armed Forces. My claim to fame was that I could get celebrities' autographs. *Moby Dick* had just been released in one of the English speaking houses and John Huston was coming over for dinner. Chris Hatchell asked me if I would get Huston's autograph. I owed Chris a favour because he was always very generous about slipping me a ticket to the 'Maag' showings and I would have missed a lot of films if it hadn't been for him.

This was a big event for my parents. I thought of myself as a seasoned artist in his own right, unaware that John Huston wrote his own plays, did his own painting and even was known to give a few idiosyncratic performances. Being ten years old it was hard for me to believe that anyone else could be as talented as I believed myself to be. My current concern was an impression of Laurence Olivier as Richard III. I was mesmerised by his portrait of villainy, especially since it was possible that Olivier was encroaching on my father's area of thespianic expertise. No one had been more menacing to me than my own father, until I saw the spry gracefulness of the cripple, who spoke so eloquently and murdered so deftly, with such cold-blooded clarity. Shakespeare's words may have eluded me but Olivier's characterization was completely clear.

After dinner we all sat down in the living room and Huston told a few stories as he drew me holding Nannette, our spunky French poodle. I asked Mr Huston if he would give me an autograph for my friend Chris and Huston complied, doing a drawing of a whale shooting water from its plughole. My mother asked me if I didn't want an autograph for myself and I, half feeling a need to differentiate myself from Chris and demonstrate my own artistic independence, replied that I only collected my own autograph. Huston thought this touch of bravura clever, no doubt reflecting some of his own egocentricity; he hadn't bothered to sign the drawings of me, which were done on the opposite sides of a single piece of paper.

Well, if I didn't want to get John's autograph, would I do my impersonation of Olivier for him? Mom was following up with a typical non sequitur that gave me an opportunity to act for Huston. This I was willing to do. As I hunched my back and concentrated on getting the right quality of menacing grace that had so impressed me, my audience fell silent. I moved slowly until I was face to face with pop, Huston, and my mother, which was the way Olivier had photographed the scene.

I opened an imaginary window shutter and peered in to see the king that Olivier would later dethrone. Olivier looks at the king sitting on his throne and then looks at the camera (the audience) closes the small window and looks at the camera, again his intimate audience, pauses and says, "the King will die... I hope". As I hobbled off as Olivier's Richard III, Huston was bellowing with laughter. I turned and took a bow and Huston turned to mom and dad and said, "If Larry ever sees this, he'll quit acting".

But I didn't want to be merely the cute kid performing for his parents' friends. I would have preferred Mr Huston to have offered me a job, although I wasn't auditioning for him in any formal way. I had auditioned for the film *Boy On A Dolphin*; I remember trying to read the words in a dark room for the producer. I didn't get the part. My reading wasn't very good and Alan Ladd didn't like me playing with his son David, either. Those were the buttons I understood when Ladd burst into our dining room and quickly collected David, upset that he didn't know where we had gone to, although we had explained our departure while he was talking to someone. We thought that he had heard us. Maybe there was no connection here between my not getting the part and Alan Ladd's anger. In later years I would remember once driving out with my dad to visit Huston on the set of *The Red Badge of Courage*. I was five years old then and the drive was a long journey from where we were living to Calabasas where Huston was to be filming. I remember the heat of the day and when we arrived I saw blue figures in a field of summer weeds. It was an eerie landscape as no one was there. The figures that I saw were stuffed dummies. This image and the silence inspired a large painting of soldiers fighting Indians, which I dedicated to Mr Huston. I would have enjoyed acting I think; I did a lot of it offstage. Making a painting in a way is acting for the muses, inviting inspiration to play with you.

Several years later, I was fortunate to see Sir Laurence Olivier in a production of *Titus Andronicus* in London. After the play ended arrangements had been made for me to meet my idol. I stood in the dressing room in a state of shock to be actually so close to the person I had seen in *Richard III*, *Hamlet* and *Henry V* while my mother related the anecdote with Huston's comment. Sir Larry laughed at this and addressed me, "Michael, please give me a few more years". I had been just as surprised to hear the story as Olivier was. I felt embarrassed even though Olivier had been pleased. He went on to say that he loved the city of Venice, where my mother said I had wanted to go to see Olivier as *Titus Andronicus*. I had been willing to sleep on a park bench. Olivier was very gracious to my mother and me. We left feeling privileged to have had a glimpse of the man on the other side of the curtain. These charming events did occur. They were the lovely gifts.

Growing up in Europe and in the city of Rome, which was my home for six years, gave me a feeling for humanity I'm sure I would have missed anywhere else. It wasn't only these special visits from my parents' talented friends, it was the ambience of day-to-day living. I loved to explore Rome. I went for long walks along the Tiber River, from the Parioli Hill to Vatican City, passing all kinds of people going about their business. I felt very protected by the Italians. Toni on the other hand, going to an Italian school around the corner, must have felt alienated. But we did do routines for mom when dad was away acting. Toni is a fine comedienne. Her timing is brittle and endearing.

On Saturday mornings I went to see if there were any new antiques available at my friend's shop, Rein-Rein, which faced the Spanish steps. He always gave me the best deals with my allowance. I had fallen in love with collecting antiquities after my first visit to the Roman Forum. I got my parents keen on this idea and they took me to an auction where I was able to buy an entire collection of ancient jugs. Everyone there thought it so charming that an American boy should be interested in such things that nobody bid against me. This kind of graciousness was very customary in those days. It was in Rome that I began painting and sculpting. After a series of paintings based on Cyrano de Bergerac (I was in love with his persona and his nose) I made a handful of oils after Picasso's colourful Dora Maar portraits. I religiously copied Modigliani's exquisite profile portrait of Lunia Czechowska which was purchased at my first one-man show by the owner of the Residence Palace Hotel. After my exhibit, I set to work on a group of paintings of the fountains of Rome. Amerigo Tot, the well-known sculptor, gave me my first clump of clay. But I think I got more pleasure from taking apart my mechanical toys and reassembling the wheels and springs. I recall having made a rooster, which I exchanged for antiquity with Prince Massimo, who had married a beautiful actress. His family went back to early Roman history.

The prince was in the swimming pool business but his heart was in collecting Etruscan vases. Farmers who often found treasures while ploughing their fields knew that they could go to Massimo and sell him their findings. Since he was royalty he was permitted to collect and to dig for such objects. One afternoon while we were all enjoying a lunch in the courtyard of his villa outside of Rome, a farmer brought him a bag full of pieces that looked as if they came from the same vase. Massimo was not interested in this collection of fragments so he offered it to my father. Amerigo pieced together what he could and years later in London the chief restorer at the British Museum, Mr Beasley, did a superb job in finishing up what Amerigo had started. We were gifted with a beautiful neck amphora revealing Hoplite and archer leaving home and on the reverse side Dionysus and maenads. Black silhouettes, figures painted on a red background. I loved studying their graceful presence and sharing my admiration of the sophisticated drawing. Contemporary artists often borrowed their concepts. A window into Greek history 500 years before the birth of Jesus Christ and numerous periods in Picasso's art.

When Jim had come by for pancakes that my mother had made for us, he stood admiring the vase as well as the other artefacts we had brought back from Italy in 1957. They were all placed in a showcase that my mother had gold leafed. I had turned on the interior light to illuminate our collection. He was quite amazed that I lived with such beauty. There were other art treasures in our home but the neck amphora was what impressed Jim the most. He stood gazing at it for some time.

11

Behind A Curtain Of Flannel Pyjamas

One summer, Tom, Sean and I were in Switzerland at Ranger Camp. Tom and Sean were counsellors, older boys I knew from Rome. Each of the Gervasi brothers meant something special to me. I spent much time with Tom who tutored me in English and mathematics. I idolized their style, their seriousness of purpose and graceful manners. They also gave me a strong feeling of self-confidence as if they expected great things from me. But in spite of their presence at the villa, our camp in Glion, it was a hard summer for me. I wasn't getting along with anyone at camp. I hadn't brought my glasses with me so I flubbed at baseball. The girls pulled down my pants for writing dirty words on their mirror in lipstick. The boys made fun of my routines and I always got blisters on the hikes that we took. The one area of success I had was with telling ghost stories. These were sort of stream-of-consciousness tales that I pieced together spontaneously as the fog rolled in while we rested in a shed before descending the mountain. The stories usually incorporated tales that had been told to me, which I elaborated on by adding unconventional nuances and twists in the plots, which I stretched out, trying to squeeze as much attention as possible.

Back at camp one afternoon the counsellors decided to have a storytelling contest. For this event I supplied my story, *The Treasure Hunt*, with a map, that I purposely held upside down, along with a pair of opera glasses that I also wore upside down as I told my tale. The characters in the story included Albert Einstein and my version of his theory of relativity, which somehow factored into the search for the gold mine, place of mine, peace of mind. My shaggy-dog tale made an entertainment of my reality. I was trying to explain my life in metaphors. I was miming reality. Maybe Einstein would work out a new theory of relativity for me. I had plenty of material to choose from, which I did according to how I needed to move the plot along. At least I was safe telling stories. But not having my glasses made me remarkably accident-prone. I walked into a parked car, fell through a board, and banged my knee a few times. I was always being bandaged up. My mother had said that she had forgotten her glasses one summer and that her eyes had gotten better. I was hoping for the same results, but the only thing that improved was my swimming. Summer is the season when I come alive. The winter work is done and I can spend time experimenting, having adventures or improving myself. This habit began after I learned to swim in natural waters; lakes, streams, oceans and seas. It is also a more public period for me. A period when I re-adjust to the world around me, people and events.

Dad came to pick me up and was very pleased with my ability to do a hundred yards; he too had been a good swimmer. We left camp together and went to get my sister who was at another camp where they only spoke French. Toni was about four-and-a-half years old at that time and somehow she had forgotten all of her English and didn't recognize dad or me. My father spent the afternoon with her sitting on a hill conversing, she has a photo of them together I remember seeing. Miraculously by evening, the strange child we went to collect once again became my sister. This may have something to do with the fact that she puts herself entirely into the present. And like the dolphins, as I have pointed out, she looks to her day-to-day living. She had learned her lessons. In Switzerland, I remember that papa and I bought some water pistols and went running after each other firing away across a bridge. It was one of the few times we ever boyishly played together. We had fun but he got the last shot. Years later we were up at Big Bear in California and he managed to throw the last snowball. He hid it away just like he had saved the water in the pistol. He was sneaky that way. It gave him a thrill winning. I hadn't learned the lesson from the water pistols, but I did have fun playing. Maybe that is more important. Obviously, my pop was also telling me to look deeper, but I never did take reality at face value. Many times that is all that there is to face: a mask, nothing hidden or especially profound. Reality can be superficial as well.

We left Rome when I was thirteen. The two most precious memories that I was leaving behind would be my lost romances. I had lost Elizabeth Trohill to David Brice and France Brunnel I had abandoned, being twelve years old at that time. There are times when all of us would like to return to a moment of our pasts and recreate things differently. If I had the chance to turn back the clock, to adjust the elements of my life, I would choose to do so the summer that I met France, and go forth from age twelve with her near.

L'École de L'Humanité is nestled in the woods above Lake Lucerne, in the German part of Switzerland. This sanctuary is where I met France. The school is essentially composed of a single chalet up the road from the village where the train stops and where we spent our allowances buying chocolate and sausages to supplement the vegetarian diet. This was a small camp, much more intimate than Ranger Camp. There were less than thirty kids there but they came from all over Europe. I roomed with an American boy who had come from Paris and had been at camp for a while before my arrival. Tacked up around his bunk were cartoons he had clipped out of the

New Yorker magazine. He had a small library in fact, which he created by tucking the books between the slats that held up my bunk. Among his collection was an anthology of Damon Runyon stories, which I began to read. I was delighted with Runyon's use of the language. "Furthermore, I wish to state…", I got a big kick out of that and used it as an introductory bridge for my own stories about the kids in Rome. These adventures featured our activities playing in the ruins re-enacting some of our favourite movies and my observations about tourists or the sexual discoveries that I was taking notes on. Often I would dictate to my mother, who left spaces between the paragraphs so I could make illustrations.

My roommate and I both considered ourselves men of the world and often sat up late discussing the worries of the world and how we might solve them. We had our own worries, too. At his suggestion I stopped showing up for the morning exercises, which consisted of running through a misty forest and then taking a plunge into the icy cold pool filled with water from the stream that ran through camp. This was the invigorating dénouement that really put me off the whole process. Just putting my foot into the water it froze. Nobody seemed to mind our not being there and in fact the camp people were very freethinking and left it up to us to design our own activities. It was run by a sharp, tiny lady who arranged all the pertinent matters and settled all our squabbles. When my friend Peter left his precious sausage out on his bureau and her cat had eaten it, Peter asked me to talk to her about it, as he had no more money to replace the sausage. He was afraid to speak with her since the camp was supposed to be vegetarian. She just said that he would have to be more careful next time and that she had no intention of reimbursing him.

Her husband was the founder of the camp, or the school, I should say, but he was very old and had projects to do that were more important than putting in an appearance. He did, however, ask to meet me for some reason and he showed me a postcard that he had recently had from an old friend, Albert Einstein. He read the card to me, which expressed contrition for having helped create the atomic bomb. The founder of the school further explained that it was the guilt Mr Einstein felt that had caused him to lose his will to live, not age.

After drifting away from French lessons and woodshop I met a counsellor who was a German actor and we decided to do a play. That would be my activity and we worked on it together. The play was essentially his creation, a pantomime history of the ideas behind the founding of the school and a visit from a benefactor. Not exactly what you might call a theatrical venture, however it was something to cheer us up. I was the star and added my own touches.

Along with the play I recited one of my favourite poems that I had learned back at school in Rome, *My Native Land* by Sir Walter Scott. It's a demonstratively melodramatic piece of flag waving and I gave it my all.

> Breathes there the man, with soul so dead,
> Who never to himself hath said,
> This is my own, my native land!
> Whose heart hath ne'er within him burn'd,
> As home his footsteps he hath turn'd
> From wandering on a foreign strand!
> If such there breathe, go, mark him well;
> For him no Minstrel raptures swell;
> High though his titles, proud his name,
> Boundless his wealth as wish can claim;
> Despite those titles, power, and pelf,
> The wretch, concentred all in self,
> Living, shall forfeit fair renown,
> And, doubly dying, shall go down
> To the vile dust, from whence he sprung,
> Unwept, unhonour'd, and unsung.

Sir Walter Scott (1771-1832)

I must have put the essence of my situation together. It would seem as if this poem were a conscious choice I had made to declare my loyalty to the country of my birth, perhaps suggested by my parents. I think it was the declarative tone of the poem which appealed to me, the feeling of wanting to belong had caught my attention. I have no memory of choosing it to defend myself and yet it was a shield of a poetic nature. After all, children are sensitive to the moods of their parents and an unconscious need may have led me to *My Native Land*. If words were indeed more powerful than the sword, well then sir, I was in, and so like Cyrano, I could end my refrain with this thrust home.

This was all performed in the reading room and the whole camp came out to see it. France Brunnel was in the audience and she approached me after we had finished. She was fourteen and I was twelve. She had a pretty, long face and a high forehead. Her hair was thin and fell below her shoulders. She was quite enthusiastic about my acting abilities and she suggested that we borrow the old wind-up Victrola and have a picnic in the woods. She packed a small lunch and I selected a few records, American jazz 78s. It was very romantic. We strolled up through the woods until we came to a small clearing. We found wild strawberries and the grass was thick and comfortable. We listened to the jazz and picked at our lunch and the wild strawberries. France spoke with deep feeling about her life in Paris. She loved going to the theatre and she loved poetry. She said that I should come to Paris, I could stay with her. She would teach me French and we would have an incredible life seeing plays and reading poetry together. She felt I had great ability as an actor and she wanted to help me. The ironic thing about this is that I think that if I had gone to Paris, my parents would have supported my passion. It was not that incredible, after all. If I had been more secure about my abilities and my desires to achieve recognition as an artist, I think they would have accepted our experiment, at least for a year.

In the meantime, France took me under her wing. She insisted on darning my socks and tucking me in at night. She roomed just above me and would sneak down the outside ladder to kiss me goodnight. Sometimes I went up to visit her. We talked about everything, while she sat in front of a mirror pulling her brush slowly through her long hair. I peeked at her delicate little breasts that bounced happily behind the curtain of her flannel pyjamas. If I had a chance to turn back the clock, I would return to her room and put my arms around her and hold her tight. We would go to Paris where we would now be together. France, forgive me, my dear! Forgive me for not answering your letters or your love. I should have gone with you instead of disappearing. You understood, better than I, what life is all about. Would that I were thinking like Romeo and Juliet I might have presented myself to the film director François Truffaut.

12

Tripping With Jim

Venice – in the street, we shoot the mirror. ML02

I am sitting in Venice at the kitchen table going over some of my notebooks. It is my senior year at UCLA. Outside the light is fading and Morrison pops in. Felix has something special, do I want to join him and Phil? Before time for second thoughts Jim had charmed me into his fold. He had good timing that way; I was ready for a game. We were off on foot scurrying across the alleys like Huey, Louie and Dewey Duck the cartoon images of a Disney world, on our way to the Andes to find the precious jewels hidden deep in the Inca caves. We scurried across bridges past bungalow houses amidst a labyrinth of quaint structures. The glass chimes tinkled in the wind outside Felix's bungalow. We were on the canal off Howland Avenue. Jim softly knocked on the front door. The afternoon light was as tentative as his rapping. There was no answer. Jim went around the back. I looked into the patterns moving across the water in the canal. Jim returned, he nodded; we left quietly and as quickly as we had come.

Those few moments we spent circling outside on the veranda of Felix's bungalow gazing at the water created an unforgettable feeling as if I were in Kashmir far away from LA or this lifetime. It was a passing thought, a flash, and we were on the move again. Experience is a ball of string that each of us unravels. Fate, karma, destiny, character… it is all different for everyone. Would my own life be like my donating that painting to Jim's door? Did I expect, require, demand that every gesture I make be acknowledged, put in a museum? Isn't it all a museum? Aren't we under the cosmic umbrella? Where else is there to go? Vanity. Who said it, 'all is vanity'? Life and the living of it is the thing, even if beauty needs a place to rest. I was on the move following Jim, mindlessly enjoying, not thinking about anything, just out playing with the boys.

In the distance we spotted a police car. The black and white taxi. Jim suggested we outfox them. It was a grey winter's day, no one else was out except for us; we looked automatically suspect. It was part of the game, to see if we could lose them, tease them a bit and then disappear into thin air. We crossed a footbridge to the other side of the canal, down an alley and up; we had gained time. We walked on more confidently now. They had missed us. We were now approaching the boardwalk that ran parallel to the ocean in front of a long bay of sand. The grey of the afternoon light had darkened. Along the boardwalk the palms shifted ominously in the cool breeze that was coming off the tops of the white caps foaming in the distance. Jim stopped in front of a small water fountain. I had forgotten that we had actually scored anything. Jim handed me a pill and bent down to drink some water. "I used to drink here, last summer," he intoned in a manner suggesting fondness as he tilted his head to the side. Phil and I swallowed our trips. It was time to head for some shelter. Jim suggested that we drive over to his pad, which was on Fourth Street, as there was time before the trip would hit. Back at my place we jumped into my TR3 and drove the few blocks east.

We entered a small apartment with peace-eye throw rugs and wood panelling. As I was taking inventory of the pad, Jim immediately turned on the radio, which I noticed to be a large and modern set. He was crouched down to turn the knobs. He did this very attentively; he was completely focused on the radio. Jim had knelt down as if in front of an altar. A connection was being made in this moment of intense focus. To listen was to become one with the music. Later when Jim wrote about music being your only friend, I thought of this moment and what seemed like a communion. When he sang at the Unicorn coffee house he had pressed his boot to the stand of the microphone with this same sense of intense connection. The channel would be opened and the words came up from inside his body, travelled into the microphone to explode in the amplifiers as clear words on the sea of air, carving out of the waves the words of prayer, the song, the message, his soul. When Jim kneeled to listen to the radio it seemed an acknowledgement of all beauty. The nature of his own moves opened the channels and showed me the grace of his reverence.

Phil had already disappeared into another room. I felt slightly on edge, not knowing exactly what to do with myself. Standing in the door jamb, watching Jim deftly tuning the dial, I felt out of place, trapped. There was an empty room so I decided to lie down in it and take inventory: cool down, get a hold of where I was.

Lying on the floor the feeling of discomfiture seemed to be increasing and I felt nauseated. This was a typical reaction going into a trip, but it always affected me badly. I sat up in the hopes that I would feel better. Listening to the music I heard a blurred chorus of what I imagined to be giant frogs belching and burping outside. The room was claustrophobic. I got up on my feet.

I saw Jim leaving the radio and heading out the door. "Where are you going?" I thought I was saying, but he left without responding. I followed, but he had disappeared. I felt better outside in the dark air, comfortingly wet and frothy. There was a fog, a mist that hung around the lampposts, but I could see clearly. The plants, illuminated by the streetlights, appeared violet and fleshy. A car lurched in the distance. I found myself peeing. It felt warm. How long had I been walking? Do I live nearby? I was moving unconsciously through this dark world, aware only of moving and then I turned on all the lights in my apartment. How had I found the switches? I crawled into bed feeling my kidneys: large tubes of lipstick, full of blood, full of youth, a very rich feeling, overwhelming. Is someone talking to me? Who is there?

There is only the moment; so many thoughts and experiences coming and going in a small brightly lit theatre of images. Pick one and find the past parading in front of you, aping pleasure. They all seemed to have the same weight, as if meaning had no special importance, the moments of a life being mere sculptures. The mind empties, I am here in my living room typing, having spent the day writing, sculpting, going to the post and coffee between the rain in the fresh air. I am alive, rolling and unrolling a thread, sound the trumpet, I am grateful, ready for a new call to arms. The memory of having the sensation that William Shakespeare came to visit me that night and how flattered I was to have him near; looking over my shoulder as he passed, looking to find a new drama. Alas, I wasn't writing anything on paper, it wasn't necessary; it was all in my mind, especially how quickly he made off with all my ideas.

Voices seemed to be coming through the radiator. Jim had forgotten to turn off the radio. What are they saying? It's in a foreign language, or is it Morse code? Damn, I should have studied that at school. What was it that Ginsberg was saying about the CIA? Is the radio taping me through the radiator? Where were my friends? What is a friend? Why did they have to kill me? I wouldn't play along? Was it a kind of new Mafia or something? What was this LSD? A secret way of recruiting people, transplanting energies into other bodies, transforming your body? Where was Jim? I was sure he could answer all these questions. Where had he gone? How had he disappeared so quickly? Was I farting? I felt better. Was it getting lighter? How long had I been wrapped in bed? Could I find my way back to the apartment? I'd wait for dawn. It was odd to feel Shakespeare's presence; maybe he thought this would make a fine play? Hamlet? I thought that the night had passed quickly. I had listened to the radiator as if it were monitoring me or I it. What a strange trip! I didn't like thinking about the CIA or hearing voices over the radiator. It wasn't amusing to live through, even if it was funny to think about later. It was a madness. And I'm not mad. A happy fool to be sure to expose myself to the wind, to see what's flying. But when you are thinking thoughts that don't feel like your own invention, then reality is another kettle of fish. That is an unholy monster of an experience, when you sense that you are not there, that it is not you who are thinking, a conscious nightmare.

Was it Jim's reality? I felt there was something almost vicious about this acid, as if it had stolen into my consciousness and made off with something. With the sun came a sense of ease and just Willy Shakes and Rock'n'Roll. The morning air was fresh and I was genuinely pleased to see other people routinely going about setting up their shops for the day's business. Passing a small park even the trees seemed pleased to see me. They appeared like sentinels, bright and peppy in the early morning sun. It was a sparkling blue morning, the first after a long stretch of grey ones. I had the impression that I was in another town. Perhaps Arles. The pine trees and the park had made me think of Vincent. A happy Vincent, the painter off to a vineyard in the morning sun before it became too brutal. I was too agitated to paint. There I was. This was the apartment. The door was open, so I entered. I called out but there was no answer. Turning around I was facing Jim, who just walked in as if that night had never existed and he was dropping in to see an old friend after a long period of absence. He threw his arm around my shoulder, delighted to see me.

"Got any grass?"

"Where have you been?" I responded, slapping the leaf of a plant as we headed toward the sidewalk.

"Don't do that; don't hit the plant."

I acknowledged his request and asked him again where he had been all night.

"Oh, I was down at the beach, listening to the waves."

"Wasn't it cold?" I asked. Jim laughed.

He laughed himself into the back seat of my TR3 and wrapped his legs around my waist. Jim was so buoyant, full of cheer. It was clear to me he hadn't spent the night listening to a radiator. The music had continued in his head, the waves playing softly. Had he composed some of his gentle lyrics about swimming to the moon and climbing through the tide?

The lyrics were clear and full, the gesture as open as his wrapping his legs around me.

I laughed and off we drove to my apartment. Jim and I bolted into the pad and sat down at the kitchen table.

"Where's Phil?" I asked.

"He'll show up," Jim quipped; he was still laughing.

Examining the grass Jim suggested that we eat it rather than smoke it. Conveniently there was a jar of honey on the table, which we opened and dipped our hands into like cubs, then rolling our paws into the grass. The grass lost its bitter taste. We were pleased at our ingenuity.

There was a knock at the door. Phil came in and he and I looked at one another. We seemed to spring apart and fly through the air, as if some energy field existed between us rendering us non-compatible. This was phenomenal, yet meaningless. Like my paranoia. It was there however, and whatever that energy field had been, it did separate us, throwing us apart as if we'd been sucked into a black hole and shot out. In the future, we would never become close friends, but for that moment, in my kitchen, we all laughed it off and

Phil joined in for our breakfast of grass and honey. The three of us sat in the small kitchen, the sky turning grey again. We gazed at each other, grunting. I had some trepidation about doing grass after my ordeal the previous night, but now I felt more secure amidst company. Nothing was said for the longest period as if we were catching our metaphysical breaths.

Then Jim broke the silence, "Shit!"

I sized this up and carefully responded mimicking his cool posture with a "Fuck."

Jim in turn gave me a long hard look and then said, "Shit." I volleyed back with "Sheet."

He felt that this needed a decisive "Fuck." I quite agreed, "Fuck."

Between our exchanges of "Shit" and "Fuck" were thoughts silently placed that indicated exactly just how the 'shit' should sound and exactly what we meant by the work 'fuck'. Indeed there seemed to be a real conversation going on between us. The weightiest bits of philosophy, our goals, our disappointments, the lovely ladies we had laid were all described in this manner, in the minutest details. The worldview itself, *die Weltanschauung*, everything lay between these two words. We had boiled it all down to a few syllables to record time. To give a simple sound the feel of a vast experience. There wasn't much beauty to this, no real elegance, rather a symbiotic embrace of the void we would have to fill to become artists. For the moment, it was a substitute, a smug comment. Vietnam and middle class sheep sat at our sidelines, but we had no money, just sad shoes and attitude.

Throughout our exchange Phil sat nonplussed. Out of the silence he began laughing, laughing like a drunken gypsy. And then Jim and I understood what we had been doing and we began laughing as well.

This moment of brightness faded. "Do you want some tea? I mean to drink," I asked. Phil thought he might have some. Jim's head was drooping. "Are you okay Jim?" He didn't answer; instead he fell into a stupor. I was concerned. I recalled that Jim had taken some tests at UCLA, that they had concluded he had *petit mal* or some such. I had thought that this was just a part of his cloak-and-dagger routine, but now I was alarmed. I reached for him and he, almost sensing my presence, raised his head.

He looked half asleep. He smiled that mischievous boyish smile, "Wanna go for a walk? I'm fine, man, hey, let's go out, c'mon man, follow me." Jim got up slowly, gracefully pulling up his body, summoning his strength. I turned off the water, which hadn't boiled yet, anxious to accommodate Jim's wish to be outside.

The mid-morning air was warm and it felt good to be out in the open without a roof binding our thoughts.

"Damn, my moccasins are still wet. I'll just slip them off." The pavement was warm.

Jim and Phil were a few paces ahead of me. I ran to catch up and decided to pass them by; I liked running. I stopped and turned, made my hand in the shape of a pistol and pretended to take aim at my companions, transforming the run into a game of Cowboys and Indians. Jim and Phil sprang into action; they drew their imaginary guns and 'scuttled up' to join me. The grey of the morning suggested an old TV serial western; Hopalong Cassidy, Roy Rogers and Gene Autry together for the first time. We were joining forces to right the wrongs of this here frontier town. Now we were cooking.

"Do you think they're behind us?" I asked Phil, who looked at Jim who answered, "Yep."

"Let's go this way," Jim indicated and pointed to the right. We were heading for the pass. They always headed for the pass.

I scouted the buildings looking for the bandits hidden between the boulders. I thought that I had spotted one; you couldn't be too careful. My horse, my legs, were in good shape, we galloped toward the boardwalk. Around it goes, cinema, young boys pretend, reality on drugs, the reel, *our* real, projection of cinema onto reality. Guns, hunting, escape, hiding out forever and ever as boys will be boys, being men; endless cinema, endless wars.

At the clearing the grey sand melded into the grey ocean. At the boardwalk the sensation of a western faded and now we were in another film, a Godard flick, cinéma vérité. We stopped in front of a mirror to examine our appearances. I drew my gun and shot at the image reflected in the pitted surface. *Dans la rue on tuais le miroir.* I heard the waves crashing in the distance. Jim and Phil were twenty feet ahead of me. They were pinned up against a doorway. I came up behind them. Jim had a bit of the Jean Paul Belmondo about him: "if you don't like the country, if you don't like the sea, if you don't like women, well man, go 'F' yourself." All said, to be sure, sotto voce, never macho, standing as tall as you possibly can and shooting from the hip like Alan Ladd in *Shane*. Jim was studying a car in the parking lot across from us, beyond the green cupola. It was the only car in the lot. The lot was closer to the ocean than we were. Jim turned to me, quizzically and tilted his head, "Hey, man, go check it out."

As I crossed over to the lot, cinéma vérité faded into the grey realities of a real street scene. I was standing twenty feet or so now in front of a sedan. I stopped, thinking it was odd for Jim to have sent me over. A slim black figure extruded itself from the passenger side. The voice of the young black man was very tender, very gentle, "do you want something, man?" The timbre of his voice came from another drug experience. "What do you want, man?" I shook my head indicating that everything was fine; somehow I did not want to break my silence. I turned around, headed back. I knew that they had been on heroin, I could feel it in his voice, and heroin was a drug that scared me. The sound of the young black man's voice made a very gentle impression upon me. I'm damned sorry I didn't open my mouth, I was scared but it wasn't as if that meant I'd take the heroin. His gentle voice had a sense of promise to it. One, two, three, four, open the door, there is no undercover man. We all uncover some aspect of reality. Nobody can take what you don't own. It's where you put things, ideas, words, they already exist. That is what the radiator was trying to tell me. Don't fall into a timid mode, keep it open. It's all the same stuff piled up on a DNA strand in different amounts, orders, signals. I could have said, "hello, how's it going?" Life is a participatory sport, so Harry, be kind to yourself and dive in. Thoughts are prayers, action is what is called for. Yeah, it wouldn't have killed me to have said "hello".

"What's up?" Jim asked secretly knowing my sense of dislocation.

"Spades ruining themselves on junk," I replied.

We walked back to my apartment; the spell of movie land had been broken. Jim decided to continue on with Phil. I climbed up the stairs and made myself a cup of tea.

13

Poetic Ammunition

Roberta was coming down from San Francisco; she reminded me of France Brunnel. Somehow I got hold of an eight-millimetre camera and filmed all the activities we did in a flowing gesture that I hoped would make a short film. Roberta combing her hair, Roberta standing in the kitchen, the spring light dividing her face in a chiaroscuro composition creating a young Renaissance Beatrice. I tilted the camera and then turned it to upright. I was a giant awakening from a snooze, quickly held captive by the blithe spirit that was softly stepping, dancing away toward the light flickering off the ocean. Flickering and fading, and Roberta walking away from the setting sun. Stepping back into indigo Egyptian light, stepping softly, softly dancing as the light disappeared. The image of Roberta dancing was no longer able to imprint itself. The final image: a soft fade out away from the light of the sunset.

My energy wanted to pour through the eye of the camera. I tried to spill light itself onto the film as I exposed it to capture Roberta approaching from the other side of a bridge. It gave me great pleasure to have Roberta visiting. The sequence I chose for myself reflected this enthusiasm. I asked Roberta to film me jumping naked in my living room. Roberta was somewhat overwhelmed by all my energy.

She was a quiet person and our lovemaking revealed our differences as well. Roberta wondered if she didn't depress me. I hadn't thought of it that way and I tried to reassure her, but she had touched on something. Away from the incense of San Francisco, the dining at Japanese restaurants, the fog, the poetic esoterica that protected us like the hills which sheltered the delicate phosphorescent glow of 'beatness'; away from these familiar surroundings, Roberta was wilting. The harsh sunlight of the

Hollywood desert was too strident for her to feel comfortable in. I knew as she sat on the edge of my bed that she would not be staying for long, but while she was with me I wanted to keep us cheerful. My determination seemed to bother her, so I backed off and we went visiting.

In a way, I was following the McClure pattern: he had taken me to visit *Jefferson Airplane* in San Francisco. I thought perhaps taking Roberta to see *The Doors* might offer a little distraction for an afternoon. We found Jim pacing in a brightly lit kitchen, pacing and grumbling. Ray, John, and Robbie tried tepidly to dissuade his anger. Roberta and I just stood there mesmerized. Jim was working things out and he didn't much care if he had an audience. In fact I think he liked having us there. I was in an up mood and not at all affected by his growling.

It was a hypnotic moment; Roberta was also transfixed. Jim pulled out a Bowie knife and threw it into the floor. He kept pulling it out and throwing it into the floor. Knife in the water, knife in the floor, cut it up, and make some more.

Come on, Morrison, show us your stuff, pull out the knife, and try to look tough. Jim and I were both soldiers. My father had fought in Washington; he had surrendered. Jim's father was an admiral; he was victorious. Both Jim and I were creating new armies, soldiers who could deal with the lies that each of our fathers had to tell themselves. Probably that they hated doing what they felt they had to do. That was the bond that made our friendship so compelling. We recognised each other's hats. Jim was scratching his way up. Hamlet with the bare bodkin, or was it Jim Bowie defending the Alamo? Remember the Alamo! Jim was working up the anger. Throwing the knife into the floor.

Did you remember to bring the ammunition, asshole? Morrison wasn't using any words. The dialogue was in the action. All the stops had been pulled out and the anger was flowing. Did you remember to bring the ammunition, asshole? The world is not ready for peace, asshole. Here come the planes. Not Exupéry, asshole, but American planes and we're gonna whup the Russkies. Yeah, we're goin' to smash the living shit out of them. Fuck, yes. Asshole. Don't give me that Krishnamurti crap, I know an asshole when I see one. From green bucks to silverwhite smithereens, if I'm not a Yankee Doodle Asshole, then that is not an H-bomb, H. Heroin, smack heroes Hop and Hopalong and Butch Cassidy, asshole.

Me and my cowboy hat are gonna personally kill every last asshole, asshole. Flowers of Evil, degenerated French faggot asshole. Fuck you too, Baudelaire. Fuck you, T.S. Eliot. Tough shit, Eliot, whimper my ass, asshole. Life is just like a football game, asshole. So kick off or fuck off, it's all the same. Jim kept pulling out the knife and throwing it in. The monologue was only in my mind's eye. Jim hadn't said anything. I don't know what had angered him, could be just about everything. It was an eloquent anger, an explosion we hadn't expected. It drove us away.

Ginsberg was giving a poetry reading at the Cinema Theatre. We sat listening to him chanting and sounding the small brass chimes that he held between his thumb and forefinger. I wondered what it had been like for him travelling in India. Certainly it was the place to go to put the finishing touches on one's soul. I had brought a small Etruscan shard, which I gave to someone to give to Allen. I felt I wasn't quite ready to meet my guru; I wanted to know more, I wanted to feel confident when I shook Mr Ginsberg's hand. I loved Ginsberg's poem *Who Be Kind To* which had been published along with an interview in the *Los Angeles Free Press*.

I relished the fact that the interview was made at a hot dog stand on the Strip; it added to the down-home all-American 'beat' poet image of Allen, talking about getting poetry on the radio and how Bob Dylan was really a surrealistic medicine man trying to cure a materialistic America. In a way, *Who Be Kind To* was like the 'Welcome the Bomb' committee at Bard; being kind was the answer. Being as isolated from the pressures of the world as I was, it was odd to me how everybody just didn't put down their work and go out and have a good time. A general strike, as it were. This was before all the love-ins and festivities that were to follow in 1966 and 1967. Kids were still wearing their hair short. As far as that goes, I think if I could have invited the whole world to my birthday party that Prince Toto (a comic star in Italian films) threw for me when I was twelve, no one would ever put on a helmet. Toto had surprised us with paper hats of all the remarkable creatures in the animal kingdom. We sat around transformed into lions, roosters, bears, peacocks, crows, sparrows, all of us blowing our whistles, eating cake and ice cream and having a carefree time celebrating.

    Roberta stayed a brief week and then returned to San Francisco. We never wrote each other except once when I sent her the film we had made as a souvenir. I thought back to the party where I had met her, sitting on the sink counter in the kitchen, dangling her violet stockings and looking very content about life. I had broken into her poise by way of quoting from McClure's play *The Beard*: "why don't you sit on my lap, and play with my cock?" I was drunk and she was amused. I had gone to her pad and we had made it. I had never asked her if she knew I was quoting McClure, I always felt she had intuited as much.

14

Self-Realization Center

I hadn't seen Jim for a long time. "Come on, man, come with me. Come on, come for a ride." Jim had a Thunderbird and a new set of clothing. A pretty black chick was sitting behind the steering wheel, waiting for us. Morrison looked good. There was polish about him.

"What have you been up to, Jim?"

"Checking it out, checking it out. Come on, man, I'll show you my new pad."

He motioned for me to follow him. Jim had me sit in the front seat next to the young black girl. As he crawled into the back seat I noticed that he was wearing leather slacks, boots and a turquoise shirt. His hair was longer as well.

"Julie, this is a good friend of mine, Michael. We were at school together."

"Nice to meet you, Michael. Where shall we go, Mr Morrison?"

I thought that was odd, addressing Jim so formally.

"Ah, let's go for a ride towards Malibu!" Jim's voice was soft, velvety.

"So, how's the painting world, ol' buddy?" We slipped into conversation. It seemed to me that Jim just wanted some distraction. He listened attentively.

"I've been working on this large painting of sand. Silly, eh?"

"No, man, you're down to the grains, that's all." Jim beamed, he knew what I was doing better than I did.

"Hey, how would you like to stroll around the lake at the Self-Realization Center?"

"Fine, Jim. So what's with you?"

"Ah, well, I'm singing with the group, *The Doors*. Why don't you check it out next week? We'll be at the Unicorn on the Strip, you know the club, next to the Whisky." The way Jim said 'Whisky', it sounded like a place he would take next, like a soldier sizing up a landing, it was a question of timing. The Unicorn was a pretty good score, I thought. I'd first seen Lenny Bruce there. He asked the waitress to bring him 'a coke in a condom'. It was before I knew what a condom was. There was nobody at the Self-Realization Center. Walking around the lake, having the place all to ourselves, we might have been in a foreign country. Jim and I were walking ahead of Julie.

"What's with the black chick, man?"

"Yeah, she's my nurse." Jim turned to me and looked me straight in the eyes.

"You know, when I was high on acid once, I looked in the mirror. Only the eyes were beautiful." It was like what Merezhkovsky said about Leonardo da Vinci, 'the eyes are the mirror of the soul'. We were in an alcove. Jim sat down and I joined him. There was a breeze coming off the lake that combed the water, beckoning to us for attention.

"This seems like a good place."

"A good place for what, Jim?"

"An afternoon snort. Just a peek into another country."

"Let's go chat with God," Jim uttered calmly as he got up slowly, facing the path. "Come on, man, we'll walk with Jesus, okay?"

That was fine with me. I needed to move. I felt uneasy. Jesus, what a way to live. "How do you feel, man?"

"Just like the Doc ordered, all warm and battened down in the hatches," Jim laughed. "Look at all this nature, just look, so beautiful." Jim walked slowly, planting his feet securely on the dirt path. "This is my favourite spot, man. This is where I like to talk to the man. You know, we have a lot to talk about."

"Do you want to be alone for a while?" I asked, concerned.

"Oh, it's okay." He looked radiant. "Hey, wanna go to Watts with me? I bet you've never been to that side of town. It's nice there, soft." He had planted his intention neatly.

"I don't know, Jim," I was scared.

Jim laughed. His eyes seemed less liquid.

"Hell, man, by the time we get back to the car I'll be my old self.

C'mon, we'll have a good time. Don't be such a big chicken shit, man, I'll make sure that you get out okay." I knew Jim was right. I was being an old maid.

Jim was like a cat. Whatever happened, he would always land on his feet.

Driving down the Coast Highway, breathing in the salt-fresh air, I felt more at ease. Jim was jovial. In fact I felt swell myself.

"I'm having a great time. We're going places. You know, you ought to manage us. Maybe use some of your dad's know-how or whatever. You'd have a good time, too, lots of tail, right Julie?"

"Mmm hmm," Julie echoed. She was smiling too.

I got uptight at this suggestion. I could see my painting career going out the window. "I don't know, Jim. Let me think about it. I mean, managing isn't my bag."

"Nothing to it, kiddo, we get you a dynamite secretary and an office, that's about it, just looking after the store, man." The image did have an appeal, but...

We were now on the Santa Monica Freeway heading into the city. "Let me think about it, Jim. Definitely I'll come and see you at the Unicorn. Let me take it from there, okay?"

"Sure man. Whatever you say." Jim was disappointed at my reticence. We went to a home somewhere near USC; it wasn't quite Watts, but we were the only white people at the barbeque. Everyone was relaxed. There weren't any bad vibes.

"Isn't this nice man? Homey-like?"

"Yeah, Jim, how do you know these people?"

"This is Julie's family. She's just checking in, making sure everything is OK."

It occurred to me then that Jim had fabricated all this; the car was Julie's, she was helping Jim's game. I would have thought that Julie would have resented catering to Jim's game. But I was wrong. She enjoyed it. It was fun for her, too, pretending to be his chauffeur and nurse. Jim said he knew of another party and that we should check it out, there would be booze and lots of girls. Julie took us to a fraternity party closer to USC. It was dark by now and the party was under way. I wasn't in a party mood. Seeing Jim stoned disturbed me. It lingered. Jim, however, was having a great time. He looked like a sparrow hopping about, chatting it up, appearing and disappearing. Julie and I started talking.

"How long have you known Jim?"

"Well, we met last week, I saw him in a club in Santa Monica. He was great, so I talked with him. He's a good boy."

Jim spotted us and motioned for us to join him. "Have some of this weed. It's psychedelic, really." A girl came up to me and started talking to me. It was hard for me to understand what she was saying with the Rolling Stones playing inside my head. She was very pretty and seemed pleased to know me. She began to walk towards the door and I followed her. Outside, the stars were bursting with light. The girl said her name was Jenny and she asked me where I lived. "Venice, I'm here without my gondola." Before I knew it we were driving down the Santa Monica Freeway. Jenny had her hand on my leg and I looked at her dress. Her legs were very appealing. The car had stopped but it was not my neighbourhood.

Jenny was opening the door for me. Gee, that's nice, I thought. Her apartment was small. I was spellbound by a bouquet of flowers sitting on a beautiful polished oak table. I hadn't noticed her putting on the music; I was surprised by its presence. I think it was Satie, it was very gentle music and Jenny stood in front of me wearing a white robe. She held out her hand.

"I understand that you're a painter? I'd love to pose for you sometime." Jim had filled her in. "Do you want something to drink, some juice, or wine?"

"Listen Jenny, I, ah, I've had a big day. You're sweet and I'd like to, but I don't think I can just now, you know?"

"It's okay, Jim told me you were very sensitive. I know you're not a fag. You don't have to perform."

"I'd like to, really, but my head is in the clouds. I'm a long way away from feeling sexy. It's awful, isn't it?"

Jenny laughed and came over to sit next to me. She put her hand on my leg again. "Listen, Michael, you just relax. Close your eyes and dream away…"

There was laughter. I was thinking of Bard College, an afternoon when I knocked out the top panel to my front door and, going around to replace it, I was struck with an impulse to entertain some of my friends. I was doing a TV routine about philosophy, which I proposed was a question of how people walked. I adjusted my accent to the country I was discussing: the French, being existential, walk leaning into the future, tipsy in the manner of Jacques Tati. You see, we are impatient for knowledge and if our têtes get there before our tits, so much the better.

The Italians, on the other hand, arrive in the present with their stomachs first.

After all, the stomaco is the most important part of the physical anatomy, and therefore it is the guiding spirito. Eh, Italian philosopho is pragmatico. Pasta, basta, portfolio, isa really communicato il senso of Goddo, Esistenza, and Creation. This essence is the actual evidence of meaning, which precedes each Italian. The greater the philosopher, the bigger the stomach. Eh, eh! Clear is clear! After all, if one needs further proof of our expertise, one has only to have a meal: there is always a parade of Papa, pasta, and groups of the family. An Italian never eats alone: that would be sacrilegious. That is why the Italians believe that one is never alone with a plate of spaghetti. The fact that the Italians and the French had claimed the most impressive aspects of the anatomy of philosophy, the stomach and the head, explains why the Germans were left with the soul. That is why they are a nation always on the march looking for a good idea and a good meal. Nietzsche proclaimed that the Germans were supermen, that they could fly, even if they couldn't get a good meal. They thought to hire Wagner to write very loud operas so that they couldn't hear their own stomachs grumbling. Of course the Italians were not perfect, either: after we got tired of playing gods and goddesses and throwing a lot of parties, we made a big slip, which was to hire a young Rabbinical student to take over the act. As a result, the bread got divided. He became so good that he even managed to come up with a real showstopper: Walking on Water. Eh, too much fishing, no? It's a sad story, the end, now, so I'm gonna ask my favourite American gangster Home-free Bogarto to do his own version of the famous love poem by his drinking buddy Dylano Thomaso, eh. In America love is more important than spaghetti.

Lisping like Bogart, "thanx, kid, I think all this eating was making me heavy, uh? I think I have room, though, for a wittle wove poem." He quoted a few lines from Thomas's *If I Were Tickled By The Rub Of Love*.

I heard laughter as well?

"Oh, that's a good boy."

Where was the voice coming from? How long had I had my eyes closed? Opening them, I saw Jenny looking up at me from having my cock in her mouth. It was as if the three of us, me, my cock and Jenny's face had just run into each other accidentally. We were pleased to see each other and a bit surprised. I closed my eyes. I was riding a camel in the desert. It was high noon and the sun was blazing, but there was a cool breeze; it was an air-conditioned desert. It didn't make any sense, but I wasn't asking any questions. The voice in my head sounded like Rod Serling. We were riding to an oasis that I could see growing larger and larger. There were all these T-birds parked out front. They were all the same model, painted different colours. There was a big sign hanging between two magnificent palms. It read: 'Aldous Huxley presents The Doors of Perception, with Bill Blake, Arty Rimbaud and Chet Baudelaire on drums and the Songs of Innocence and Experience sung by…' I didn't get a chance to finish reading the marquee… "Hey, man, you're not ready for work, huh?" Work? Oh, yeah, I remember now. We were working for Jacques Overhoff spackling, spackling, endlessly spackling the reliefs that he was doing for the Mark Taper Forum. Tom was at the door. I was surprised to see that I was back at my apartment and that it was daytime.

15

Working With The Boys

I happened to be in the office of my advisor, Oliver Andrews, who was the head of the sculpture department at UCLA. He was on the phone to a sculptor who was looking for a student to help him. Oliver held the line and asked me if I wanted a job; I jumped at it. Jacques Overhoff had been commissioned to do the reliefs for the Mark Taper Forum. He had devised a rather unique way of working.

He carved 40-foot long blocks of Styrofoam with an electric kitchen knife. My job, along with three other assistants, was to spackle the surface of these nine reliefs and then sand them.

The worksite was in Sun Valley, which was a long drive from my apartment in Venice. The traffic was never bad, as we worked long hours, usually knocking off around eight at night. There was a deadline to keep and Jacques made sure we didn't screw around too much. He didn't mind if we smoked grass as long as we kept moving things along. There was a nice feeling among us. I think we all felt akin to the workers who had built the cathedrals during the Middle Ages. They too had worked as anonymous craftsmen. Bob was the foreman. Tom and a tall fellow Pete, called the 'slim bear', and I talked art, sex and politics as we spackled away. I collected the used Styrofoam chunks and carted them to the foundry I used in Venice. Alf Peterson's one-man operation was where I had had my first experience with pouring bronze. Alf was a pack rat and his yard was filled with all kinds of goodies that I incorporated along with the Styrofoam. I was playing with the idea of ready-made assemblage using bamboo as poles along with other objects. I felt no need to complete these experiments although I wish I had documented them. At the end of an afternoon's work, I disassembled my efforts and put everything back. It gave me a good workout and a feeling of purity not having to keep the works. Besides, there were plenty of other projects that resulted in concrete objects. I did a series of etchings, mostly based on my poems. I called these etching movies.

> Tom has just shot Mike
> Sheriff Allen once touched Tom's head at
> A poetry reading, The posse—the Fugs
> Will all sing down Tom, as I try to shave
> Or unmask the sheriff.
> In the desert Tom finds the pie of highs.
> Tom eats a piece,
> Bob eats a piece,
> Bobbie is shampooing her hair.
> Back at the ranch Jack (K) is petting
> My cat.
> Hollywood Blvd. took LSD
> Tom is caught with his tongue out
> B.B. Kisses François in France
> Indoor sequences were shot on a
> Busy day at Frontierland.
> The cast kiss 'n make up then exit via
> The freeway, walking
> I decide not to shave Allen
> Ciao a tutti.

Above the poem was an illustration of a gunfight and a make-believe series of mug shots of Allen Ginsberg, Michael McClure and Tom Hexdall, who had become a kind of buddy while we worked for Jacques. An arrow pointed to McClure and indicated that he looked like Rimbaud at 15, although the face was blank.

I showed one gallerist several studies in wax of Roberta sitting in a chair looking very Egyptian. He liked the work but thought it too close to another artist whom he was already handling. Also there were a few cutout abstractions in wax that were attempts on my part to make a sculpture that presented itself like a flower in bloom. One of the more bizarre oil paintings was a surrealistic portrait of my defunct TV that I painted to look like a house. Had I persisted and documented everything, there might have been a chance to break through, but funky work is always difficult. The artist would have had to have a lot of charisma and strength to pull that particular rabbit from his hat. I needed a gallery to get my 'career' going. I was naïve to think it would be so easy. A collector once informed me, "get in line fella, there are 1000 artists in front of you."

16

Spilt Popcorn

At the end of my first semester at grad school I collected together a sampling of the varied works I had been doing. At this point I had been working at home or at Alf Peterson's yard. I brought in waxes, a few oils, etchings and my book of poetry. Grads were not present when the committee made their evaluations and as it turned out they did not know what to make of my potpourri of creativity. Of course, there was no clear-cut body of work, rather a series of interesting stabs in various directions. The work was very personal and really needed a complete going-over to get the gestalt of my perceptions. I think if I had brought in everything and documented the process of work I was doing at Alf's, they would have felt more secure about having me stay on. However, they decided to drop me from school. This came as a shock. It meant that I was left open to reclassification and that I might be going to Vietnam. In light of the fact that I had done so well as an undergraduate and that this was, after all, just my first semester, which included my working for Jacques Overhoff, I thought they were very callous. In fact, I thought that they were most unfeeling to drop me in the lap of the induction centre. I was pissed. Shit, I was an artist. Even if they thought that I was full of it, how could they turn against one of their own? How could I be the darling one semester and *bête noir* the next? It made absolutely no sense. I hated them. In my eyes they were no better than Nixon, in fact, they were worse, they were artists! The hell with them!

Luckily, I was under psychiatric care at the time. This had to do with my loss of energy and incentive as a result of taking LSD. Bernard Gindes treated me with hypnosis therapy, which was a big boost in putting me back on the road. At our first meeting he said that I was just 'a master, a master of the *cop out*'. There was a great deal of truth to that. It was certainly easier to stay home and work on my projects and let the world go by. I don't think this was really copping out, but Bernie wanted to see me participating in the flow of things. He was right about that; I had withdrawn. Even Overhoff gave me pep talks. I did my work and I did it well, but who wants to be around a misanthrope? Everybody had disappointments; so I didn't get a Fulbright, so Morrison didn't want me to sing with the group, so I was dropped from grad school.

Gindes would write a letter and they wouldn't take me. I was wound up tight. I didn't trust anyone, not Gindes, not the integrity of the armed forces, no, sir. They could open the trap door at any time and I would have to kiss my brushes, my paints, my notebooks, my time, my world, bye-bye. Sitting on the wooden bench at the induction centre, having seen them ask a one-armed man to do push-ups, I knew that I had not been entirely out of my mind with paranoia. The guy sitting next to me was high on acid. All I had was Bernie's word. For all I knew the whole set-up was a plot to dispose of my creativity. Haven't you read *1984* or *Animal Farm*? You never learned to hide your feelings, you have been a bad boy and we can't have anyone around who doesn't play the game. After all, if I had played the game at school, I would still be there. During the interview I exaggerated, thinking I was confessing to all the right things. However, Bernie's letter did the trick. I had over-played my part at the induction centre but no matter, I was out. No need to celebrate my 4-F classification, I felt lucky and I'd keep that to myself.

In the spirit of True Confessions, I anonymously delivered an article about my misadventures to the offices of the *Los Angeles Free Press. Like Swift Death* was the cover story for the next issue. The preface explained that I was not signing it because I felt that I could be more direct and honest that way and also I didn't want the LAPD knocking at my door. The use of LSD had become illegal; it hadn't been when I had begun taking it. The writing in the article was clipped, straight to the point. It was a good exercise for me, one of the activities that I did to get off my duff. Also I moved back to West Hollywood and set to work making a studio out of the basement of my parents' apartment, which had been my workshop when I was attending high school. I painted three of the walls to cheer up the place; a terracotta red, a bright cobalt blue, and a light cadmium yellow. I put an ad in the *Free Press* for classes. The ad was vague enough: Tarot, Mandala, Dance, Spring, April, Sculpture… Michael 695-2458. Somewhat like a McClure poem, eh! This esoteric note brought me one student, a middle-aged dentist who wanted some help with his clay sculpture of St. Francis. My student wanted to know how to organize his creation so that he would have St. Francis surrounded by a halo of doves. We worked this out in a few sessions and my pupil disappeared. My friend Forrest came by and we played together on a clay relief, which I later cast in plaster. There were other visitors: Shelly Burton, who rented the studio for a week whilst writing an article. Jim crashed there a few times sleeping on a bench. Hal Marshall a sweet guy and a small time organizer stopped by. An assorted carnival of my friends enjoyed drifting in and out of the studio, which was a stone's throw from the hub of activity just up the road at the Whisky and other clubs like the Unicorn, Chez Paulette, The Fifth Estate, et cetera. It was a convenient hideaway.

It was Tuesday night and time for me to see Jim sing for the first time. There weren't a lot of people in the club, so I felt pretty special, as if Jim were auditioning just for me. He stood in front of the mic with one foot poised on the round base of its stand and looked out over the audience as if he were looking into the future or over a vast expanse of sea. "You know, I'm gonna tell ya about the little red rooster." Jim picked up a harmonica and shot a few notes through the mic. Then he looked up again and started to sing. He stood there, hanging onto the mic. He was talking about a ride. We were all going somewhere, and Jim was going to check it out from the front seat. He looked very eloquent, very intense, as if the fate of the nation or the world depended on how he delivered his sermon. He was mesmerising. After the show I told Jim how impressed I'd been.

"Yeah!" He looked at me hard. "Listen, ah, why don't I take you to meet this chick in the music business? I'll tell her that you're from New York and that you want us to play there, OK?"

"You mean tonight?"

"Yeah, right now." Jim threw his arm over my shoulder and we started walking towards my car.

The lady we went to see was our own age, which surprised me. It didn't look to me as if she had any power. I laid it on as best I could. "Jim, you don't have any commitments, do you?"

"Well, Ray's brother is handling that. You'd better check with him."

We were in and out of the girl's place before I knew that we had done any good.

"Hey, thanks a lot, Mike. Let's talk about you *really* managing the group. C'mon, man, whataya say?"

"I don't know, man. What about my painting?"

"Shit, man, become a Sunday painter like Henri Rousseau; he did pretty good."

I was surprised that Jim knew that much about the world of painters. I remembered the collages on his wall. But I wanted to sing, too. I thought that we could be another Beatles. That wasn't what Jim had in mind.

It was thrilling to see Jim perform. He created a tension that brought you back to see him again, to see what he had discovered in the interim, exploring the horizon.

Frank Zappa was the big deal in town at that time. Everybody went to the Shrine to dance with his band The Mothers of Invention. It was almost a full orchestra, and a dance troupe which included Vito, the sculptor I had studied with when I was fifteen. Hal Marshall thought we should collaborate on a script. After all, there were so many interesting characters around. Fellini himself would love the opportunity. Hal was keen on the idea, but he could sit down for only five minutes at a time. He was driving me crazy, so I kicked him out of the studio and put together a treatment in a few days. Hal loved the outline. I would approach Jim and he would speak with Zappa, I thought. We joked about getting John Huston to fill out our scenario and direct.

I ran into Jim up on the strip. He was being interviewed by a pesky young fellow who was gingerly querying Morrison about his artistic goals. Jim was doling out vagaries. He handed down the ideas with heavy consideration and his interviewer was lapping it all up ravenously. Jim talked about TV, how it controlled our thoughts. We were walking down San Vicente towards my studio. Jim glowed. He loved this guy kissing his ass. Jim and I ducked into my studio, leaving his admirer panting like a dog in the middle of a fuck. I read Jim my outline. All he had to offer was, "uh huh." I told him that I needed his commitment.

"Yeah, well, ah, let me know when you get Huston."

"Come on, Jim. Cut the shit."

Jim said nothing.

"Shit, man, I thought that you wanted me to help promote the group." There was a pause.

"Hey, man, I got a lot going on. I'm not into movies just now. Like I said, TV, man, mainline."

As Jim surfaced into the light of the afternoon, leaving my subterranean studio, the message sunk in loud and clear. Jim was becoming a *Rock Star*. He had carved away at the idol, sharpening his features, clarifying his character, learning how and when to draw attention to himself. I had to admire his movement. 'Beauty in art is shrewdness which makes it eternal', Jean Cocteau had observed. Nobody was awarding Jim his beauty: he was fighting for it. Every move had to be successful, more cunning, more graceful. Poetry, words, they filled in between his leaping. The Jim that had taken me to the Self-Realization Center only months ago was a smaller aspect of the person who left me that afternoon. We are all aspects, pieces beautifully matched together or not. Jim was shrewd. He was hunting survival, fame, immortality a step at a time. His brilliance lay not only with his gestures, which he controlled like a trained actor, but also with his instincts for the right direction. I went after Jim. Our friendship wasn't a pleasant ride around the park or watching the waves winking. He had wanted me to help him. It wasn't fitting into his game plan that afternoon, and I wanted him to know that it disturbed me.

"God may be fame to you, asshole, but you are a prick, Morrison," I shouted at him. Jim smiled coyly and then started up the hill and out of sight.

He had hurt me. I could accept the fact that he was becoming an idol, but I resented that he should treat me like one of his worshippers. That wasn't the basis of our friendship, a friendship that he had pursued. I was being discarded.

Time passed. Hal stopped me one day. "Come on, Marc." People often called me by my father's name when they got excited or thought the illusion of a little Mafia Magic might come their way. Maybe one day I'd have a strong enough identity to truly separate myself from my father. Hal wanted me to drive him out to a service being given for Lenny Bruce. Lenny Bruce was dead.

"What?"

"OD'd."

It was in the Valley. I knew a lot of people there.

We were asked not to give the service in the cemetery. This was rather ironic, as Bruce had posed for various photos doing his shenanigans from an open grave. Someone invited us into his backyard and Phil Spector, the record producer, said a few words. Carol, the ballerina that I knew, was walking on the roof of the tract home. All of us appeared confused, shaken. Bruce's life had been tormented with legalities concerning his freedom of speech. Bruce, perhaps more than any other poet, bathed contemporary hypocrisy in his acid bath where he stripped his victims like a piranha. If he exaggerated, he did so brilliantly; the whole world was not above suspicion. His still lifes had been hilarious—the Pope on the phone with a Mafia underling who was promising him a Maserati. Why shouldn't the Pope drive a Maserati? It didn't mean that he was going to get laid, or even that Bruce was really attacking the Pope per se. It was essentially a ridiculous image. It was making the Pope human. And when Bruce pointed out aspects of rough trade in the penal system, his homosexuals survived because of their hipness. Bruce took on the world. We were shaken, of course. We had lost a good soldier. The Hipster was gone.

Carol and I were seeing each other. She would pose for me in my studio. I made several quick studies in wax of her ballet positions. She was very devoted to her creative life, keeping to a regime of exercises and classes around the West Hollywood area, to which she would ride on her bicycle. She pedaled briskly and her long flowing scarf trailing behind her lent a circus air, a Fellini pathos to the schedule of activities that she believed would make her a great ballerina. She had a piano in her apartment bungalow, which was adjacent to Santa Monica Boulevard. Under the influence of grass and her encouragement, I spent the night playing her piano. There were moments when I thought that something cohesive and pleasant resulted from my improvising. The night passed quickly and I stepped outside to get a breath of morning air. The sky was painted a flat blue, a sparkling blue like just after a rain. Scattered across the whole of this canvas were tiny puffs of cloud. It looked as if a child had spilt popcorn. Standing on the porch, breathing the cool air, I heard a voice to my left. On the porch at the end of the bungalows was the figure of a thin person with long blond hair, wearing wrap-around sunglasses. The slow incantation that had caught my attention sounded familiar. The voice was unmistakably Jim's, but not the figure.

"Wow... isn't that beautiful? Wouldn't you say that that was beautiful?"

"Jim? Is that you?"

There was no answer.

The slim, Etruscan statue turned, drank me in and then disappeared into the bungalow. That was the last time that I was to see Jim for a while, because the following week I was on my way to Europe.

17

Boudoirs Of Young Girls

Before actually crossing the ocean, I decided to stop off in New York and visit a few friends. I had never lived in New York City, though I had visited it several times, including as an undergraduate attending Bard College. Several of my Bardian friends were now living and working in the city. Allan Kronzek had an apartment on Thompson in the West Village just above Houston. Thompson Street was the centre of the village in my mind and Greenwich Village was the heart of Bohemia. It was near enough to Cornelia Street where my mother had lived during the Great Depression when she befriended her neighbour Alice Neel, the portrait artist. My mother had run away with an older writer, Edward Dahlberg, to become a writer herself. Fanya, my mom, had a lovely voice and I always loved listening to her speak. She loved that period of struggle in the village and wrote a novel about it called *Ask No Return*. It was later optioned by Garson Kanin when she had travelled to Hollywood and found work for herself as a writer at RKO film studios.

Fanya was very fond of Alice, who had come for a job interview in the antique shop my mother was running on Madison Avenue. They became fast friends that day and their friendship lasted a lifetime. I'm sure this had a great deal to do with the passion my mother had for painting. She had saved a few of Alice's canvases from being destroyed by a jealous lover. Alice painted Fanya, who had acquired a small collection of canvases, including a portrait that Alice made of me wearing cowboy boots and holding a small red car. I remember the care my mother always took in looking after Alice's work. It was the same affection that flavoured her talks about Alice and other people she knew during those days; shrouded in dull colours, winter winds, and raw passion. My mother was always attracted to passionate people. She loved to watch me work while I painted. She wanted to know my point of view and pushed me to express it, but also cautioned me not to overpaint, but to leave something to the imagination. She said, "smell the roses but do not hold them too tightly; you only smother the creation that way."

So being on Thompson Street was like being opened up, as one opens a fresh tube of colour. I felt my enthusiasm squeezed onto a palette, running as it were through fields of sensation, inspired by what has always been so astonishing about NYC, the rooms of culture, the energy of people on the move, to be free to walk and look and feel the world change from one moment to the next. NYC was thrilling after my subterranean LA studio. From the bungalow and garden world I came to sit in the hot village apartment smelling of cats, greasy with cockroaches and surrounded by the hard grandeur of tall buildings.

My grandparents, having come from Russia, helped build some of NYC's smaller domiciles, apartment buildings uptown. That work made it possible for my mother to become cultured, and to choose to become a bohemian. When she was sixteen she went to Paris to study light opera. Inadvertently she heard the voice of Edith Piaf, which was more to her liking, so she decided to quit her own singing to look for something closer to her passion and abilities.

My mother's stories were her way of discussing the pleasures of her life. Her first visit to Paris, where she stayed on some six months, was one of her favourite memories. She remembered that in the window of a small gallery in the Latin Quarter was a canvas of a young girl holding a bouquet of flowers. Picasso had come to her attention. She arranged for herself to meet Ford Madox Ford. Their rendezvous took place in the countryside. Madox Ford was a tall man. He continually bumped his head and suffered the incontinence of a wet crotch but put out a damn fine literary magazine, *Transatlantic Review*. My mother would represent the magazine in New York. And so she was a part of the avant-garde, living in Greenwich Village where Joe Gould conducted tours of artists' studios while reciting his *Oral History of the World*. My mother would speak about her youth in a state of mild revelry, lending her disclosures the tone of great value. Her stories had an almost physical presence. It was the affection she lavished on her memories which brought them to life. There was her friend Mr Yoohoo, the sculptor who worked at the Cloisters. He was walleyed. He told my mother that he could see around corners. She would go calling on him. "Hello, Mr Yoohoo. I'm here." She was fifteen years old. She didn't know his name, probably he didn't know her name. But I got the sense they were friends, they both enjoyed a special magic, the atmosphere at the Cloisters. A larger sense of comradeship grew out of the Depression years, survival and the fight for self-expression were a part of the family of man so to speak. This was the sense I hoped to recapture or feel, being on Thompson Street even momentarily.

Naturally, mere proximity to a moment in history is not a creative accomplishment in itself, but it can be a creative way to find the beginning of a project, or help sustain oneself. My own first extended stay in Paris reflected those feelings. I was happy making a series of ten etchings in a tiny atelier on rue Françoise Miron. I learned that Mozart had lived just down the block; I pretended that we were neighbours. It reminded me to keep what I was doing

energized in a lively and light fashion. So the proximity gave me a certain attitude. I very much loved that period of six weeks in 1984, crossing the Seine each day near Notre Dame, traversing Île de la Cité, and Pont Louis Philippe. A morning stroll to that Atelier in late summer weather is not easily surpassed in graceful reflections. The symbolic was the actual. The stone bridges, the swaying of the tall trees lining the banks of the Seine, their leaves of green-yellow rustling in the wind above the rushing waters that reflected them; it all had a certain melody, an elegant beauty that I could compare with Mozart.

A man is selling ice cream from a small cart and a beautiful woman wearing clean shoes passes. Further on there is the smell of hot coffee, a young couple are having their morning croissants. At the corner an old woman is painting a street scene, I stop to look. It is rather good, I'm pleased for her. I hear a spoon on a saucer as I begin to cross Pont Louis Philippe to enter the Marais area. The white clouds above me are also swimming in the Seine cut by a passing barge.

Paris has its own sense of colour. The grey buildings create fine backdrops of greys where the colours can breathe. The light of Paris is a northern light, a silver light. There are many dark colours, blues, violets, greens, enamels painted fully saturated… glistening in the snug assuredness that pure colour demands. The glitterati are aware of this magic, this detailing, making a bouncy reality of shopping.

This simple consideration gives way to the more sophisticated environment of a square like Place de Furstenberg. Delacroix located his studio above this quaint square perfect for two lovers or the pure beating heart of innocence. It is quaint in an elegant informal slightly cock-eyed manner. An iron bench and a tree sit waiting on a small island marooned in this ancient world. It's a perfect place for a poetic 'happening', a perfect park for one person. The perfect spot to read a Rilke poem or Emily Dickinson. I am trying to mix my feelings for this tiny world to its sense of grace. This grey is a cello. And that is Paris: a world of endless tonalities. In very different houses there are the studios of very different artists, like Maison Rodin or Brâncusi's studio (now removed to a freestanding spot outside the Pompidou Centre) and La Ruche where Chagall, Soutine, Lipchitz, and other refugees found a sanctuary. There is Le Bateau-Lavoir in Montmartre where Picasso painted *Les Demoiselles d'Avignon*. I had lunch with a woman who had owned the building; she lived in a Le Corbusier built for Leo Stein. She was an extraordinary cook. Each place in Paris is its own world. I understood better the journey of the *Little Prince* by St. Exupéry because everyone in Paris is looking for a home for their rose.

Paris is a stage; each of us cast in our own movies, creating in our minds our own cinéma vérité. That is the pleasure of Paris: her atmospheres. Stations of the Cross, the possibility of poems or a list of things admired. In the park Champ de Mars, the imaginary proprietor is Ray Bradbury, who points the way to a bank of lights arranged in rows of suns to illuminate the Eiffel Tower. This world is secluded by bushes and trees, but there is a park bench and a streetlight placed on the pebbled arena as if waiting for the arrival of an actor. My audience was a fellow artist I met at the etching atelier. Françoise's voluptuous nature was depressed; she needed a mentor or someone to hustle her paintings. I'd been to see them at her studio and she had come to visit me. I invited her out for a treat.

That summer in Paris I had an attic studio with one window the size of a small TV that overlooked the Seine. We had a glass of wine and decided to walk. Walking in Paris is the usual therapy. We went to the Champ de Mars. And so my performance in the Champ de Mars near the lights that illuminated the Eiffel Tower was for Françoise. It all came together nicely for her large sad eyes and my words... some borrowed from Dylan Thomas and others from that moment. Her chocolate eyes told me it was not enough to cut through her nervousness.

I began my performance facing Bradbury's suns.

"Once there was an artist who stood at the edge of the world to whisper to his audience of imaginary friends, be amazed by shapes of clouds, the sound of words. Now colours come dance on my poor man's palette. This lady is sad, requires new jewels, a dance at the sea, the tip of my hat, a smile, a cheer, a flower, a cat."

We walked on across a vast space and then crossed the Seine and had a coffee. She didn't have a clue about what to do about her art or herself. She stopped coming to the atelier so I didn't get involved with her, but found another project. Perhaps she is like my mother's Mr Yoohoo at the Cloisters in NY, someone who stirs pleasure when you think of them, and you wonder if her life is more settled. To be an artist alone in this world dependent upon one's own art to provide a living is almost the most difficult or the most providential path anyone can choose. But there is also faith that the universe wants you to be happy. So, paint on Françoise and one day he or she will find you. In my case my mother became a kind of guardian of my own passion for painting, a passion to express in colour and form the voluptuousness of life.

For the moment I was in New York and my friends Alan and Bebe were going away for a few days to get out of the muggy weather. I could use their apartment providing I fed their cat. I was, as Henry Miller had put it, 'cunt struck' at that time. I met a beautiful Irish girl at the Museum of Modern Art, a perennially happy hunting ground for culture and 'cunt'. She lived on the Upper East Side and worked, as I recall, for a literary agent. She was very interested in literature, which happened to be my middle name: Mr Sterne, 'don't ya know'. She was a beautiful girl, radiant, buxom and blonde. Her apartment was rather sparse, each object was carefully displayed. They were significant keys to the stories about her family that entertained us while we sipped our gin in her living room. At the end of a few chapters we popped into bed for a good healthy go at it. I loved it. It was the first time I really had eaten pussy. It was good, sweet, wet, clammy. She got very excited and it gave me pleasure. Then we were eating each other, devouring each other, the moon and the sun enveloped in white, hot white and cool white. I mounted her and we rocked, rocked until the floodlights went on in the ballpark, all the players came out and the crowds cheered. There were flashes of blood, white bones, darkest Africa lit up like a penny arcade. God, it was so good lying there afterward in her sweet wet flesh feeling the oceans, the stars and the planets all at rest.

In the morning we agreed to have lunch. I wanted her to meet my Uncle Marty who was a writer. I thought it would be fun. Marty was as taken with her as I. Fool that I was one dessert was not enough. Later that evening I found myself drinking an exotic concoction at the White Horse Tavern. I was in the company of a rotund lass whom I had met in the Village getting a change of clothes. We had gone with a few of her friends for a drink and I was spouting Dylan Thomas in the Inn where my favourite master of words had gulped down an entire trough of beers that had sent him to heaven. The bartender must have seen me as an obnoxious know-it-all, wagging my tongue as if I had been there in person with Dylan in 1953. My outpouring continued from the subway to a bracing ride sailing into the night waves and stars on the Staten Island Ferry. Eventually I found myself in the arms of her island of flesh. This too was full-blown. Holding her breasts I felt like the tortoise beached on a Galapagos isle dropping the eggs into the sandy shores of a wet flower.

The New Yorkers put up with me, smelling of semen, riding the buses in the sweltering summer, dashing between my love beds; a burly bear unwilling to settle at one site for too long. While the women worked I looked up old friends for lunch. I devoured the museum walls and cooled my heels in the movie theatres before the bells rang at five o'clock, then I would return to sipping gin and caterwauling about the merits of Redon, the deep wet blues of Matisse, the Glory of the Cock... the garden in Sochi of Arshile Gorky and how supreme it was to be in New York swimming in the noisy energy, the cacophony of life that must have inspired Gershwin. I left New York freshly baptized in the effluvium of Thelonious Monk mounting the stage and filling us with the meaty sap of jazz. I was bathed in the chambers of MoMA, the boudoirs of young girls and the endless smells of a city cooking the rapturous ingredients of life.

18

Adventures With Don Quixote

Madrid is in the centre of Spain atop a plateau that bakes you in the dry summer heat. The only sensible thing to do was to stay at the pool, which was several blocks away from my parents' apartment on Hurtado de Mendoza. My sister Toni was working in *Camelot*. Toni was happy to be in Spain where she had been with my parents for the last six months. It was the first time I realised she had become a young woman. Our four years difference put a distance between us, we really didn't have a bond in letters or long conversations, I blame myself for not developing a warmer relationship. I might have asked the questions. When I arrived in Spain I scratched around to find work as an actor as well. I had sent my parents a copy of *Like Swift Death*, which impressed a few of their friends including Jim

Hannagan, a scriptwriter. He wanted to meet me and after giving me the once over said I should think about writing and forget about acting, which was, as he put it, 'a dog's world'. He had worked for John Wayne and the 'Duke' in his opinion was no more than 'an overgrown sissy'. I'm not sure what this had to do with me except Jim really liked my writing. I hadn't much thought about that métier. Mom suggested that I visit Peter Beses, the editor of the *Castellana Hilton Magazine*, for whom she had written articles. The magazine was a very nicely put together affair designed to soak up loose moments and point out some of the interesting goings on in town for visiting Americans. Peter thought I was too young but his wife was keen on the idea, so Peter gave me the go ahead. I could do a few pieces on Spanish artists.

Paco Baron, a tall Don Quixote who spoke English with a deep voice, became the subject of my first article for the Hilton magazine. He had learned English while studying art in America. His studio was a whimsical affair partially carved out of a hill. There in the company of other ramshackle properties, his 'barrio' butted up against the tall, modern structures growing up all around the medieval citadel of Madrid. Paco's studio was filled with works of all media. He was a carver of wood and stone, a modeller of wax and clay, and he also welded humourous personages out of varied odds and ends including typewriters. Paco made use of everything. On trips along the highways of Andalusia he put the tooth of his chainsaw into the trunks of large fallen trees. Sputtering under Goya skies, he carved away large chunks roughing out the form and reducing the bulk weight, so that at a later date he could return to pick up his monolith and drag it back to his studio for finishing. Everything was useful for him. Even garbage was gathered to be used for armatures. Covered in plaster, these forms lay around the studio waiting for completion.

Running central throughout his work was the theme that most inspired him. The mysteries and potent wonders of his favourite food… GARLIC. Garlic was the one salubrious food that provided him not only with health but also with inspiration. Cloves of garlic were enlarged, made into floral forms that stood in heraldic clusters of polished bronze, saluting daylight like the bush of life itself.

Paco, like Quixote, found this windmill everywhere. At Cuenca, a hilltop town between Madrid and Valencia, is a forest amid monolithic boulders that had been carved millennia ago by the Mediterranean. The whole area was at one time under the sea. Paco found a good-size stone that also resembled the magic diamond shape of which he was so fond. In the village of Cuenca there is a Museum of Contemporary Art located in a not so ancient 'hanging' building. This villa is composed of small whitewashed rooms in which one or two works are displayed; therefore the viewer is made to feel intimate with the art. It was a unique experience to be able to breathe in the aesthetics of one artwork at a time. Leaving the museum, Paco stopped to talk with an old woman dressed in black. As he chatted with her about her ailments I thought of Picasso's portrait of his mother who also was wearing black. All over Spain one saw these 'black widows', many were young and many had lost their husbands in the Civil War.

Spain was exciting for me. Attending bullfights, I understood what had impressed Hemingway's notion of the sport, facing the danger of a beast with grace. Walking through Granada I happened to see a very beautiful young woman traditionally dressed. She might have stepped out of a Goya painting. How shocking it was to see her and how special. The 'hip' scene had already drifted to Madrid via London. Watching her cross the plaza didn't seem like such a rare occurrence at the time, but in the three years that I lived in Spain I never again saw a young woman who was so graceful, elegant or beautiful. Perhaps it was a glimpse into the past. It was a transcendent moment. Beauty is always a surprise and always the gift in both art and life. The Catholic Church of Spain still exerted an almost medieval hold on sexual mores: their youth dared not even flirt with the notion of pre-marital sex. The power of the church had so convoluted this temptation that it ruined my chances to have an affair, especially with a 'good girl'. The idea of going to a whore never occurred to me and under the umbrella of such an ambience my sexual drive faded during these first few months of a Castilian life now filled with other activities.

19

Magical Dancing Trees

One day greeted me with a lovely surprise: the presence of a former LA girlfriend, come to study guitar. Sally was also a friend of my sister so the three of us shared our time. Sally and I had had a so-so relationship back in LA. Perhaps romantic Spain would put a little gusto into the works. Concurrent with Sally's arrival a school chum from Bard showed up, Peter Witonsky. It was decided that Sally, Toni, Peter, my mother and I all go to Paris. Sally and I were just warming up to each other. We had leaped into bed and out again but it was just beginning. Paris would be an even more romantic site. Going up on the train Peter began to enjoy picking on Sally. This wasn't a very good start for our excursion. He seemed contemptuous of her manner, which she placed slightly above us. They were both a bit snobbish and competitive about it. Mother chatted on with Toni and arbitrated occasionally between the quips that eventually gave Peter the upper hand, being that he was a bully as well as abrasive. Sally was hurt. Toni defended Sally and I looked out of the window at the linden trees thinking of my next project, a series of lithographs on Joyce's *Ulysses*. That was my main reason for going to Paris. I would both buy the 'banned' volume and research the background of his Paris.

How beautiful Paris is! It struck me immediately. There was a chill in the air and the smell of roasting chestnuts. And the colour. How black and white Spain is next to Paris. Even the language sparkles. Paris is a perfect woman: she intoxicates everyone, charms everyone by having put aside something special, something personal for each of us, mysterious. She is a woman whom you follow from the broad boulevards, from the spacious, tree-lined plazas, into quaint streets waiting for you in Montmartre or Montparnasse. At the end of your excursion there is a bedroom, and she will always be there waiting, she is Paris.

Near Place Odéon as rue Monsieur-le-Prince feeds into it was a record store. I remember it because I hadn't seen a record store all the while I'd been in Madrid, so it was novel, like Paris itself; a touch of colour, a flowing scarf. Featured in the window display was a Doors album. I dashed in. Although I didn't have a record player, I did want to see what songs they were singing. The cover was a montage, enough to recognize Jim, his head photographed as a floating orb in a black universe. It was a black and white Hieronymus Bosch. I was familiar with some of the titles. Jim's big night at the Whisky flashed to my mind, when he sang *This Is The End*. When we had all been paralysed by his words, breaking through the nightmare echoing the Greek myth... wanting to kill his father and to fuck his mother. That moment was now immortalised on a disc, a piece of plastic you placed on a machine and as it turned, words and music came alive. But, as I had no record player, I could only visualize Jim standing in the shadows of Plato's cave, bringing Prometheus' torch right up to our minds' eyes. The disc was a reminder of our choices, graceful with love, a naked adoration for life, each day an artful greeting. It gave another aspect to my Paris, a graceful salutation from Jim.

Walking up rue Monsieur-le-Prince heading to the Hotel Stella, famed as the 'hip' hotel where Corso wrote, I was walking with Joyce. He had proved algebraically that the ghost of Hamlet's father was Shakespeare. Peter resembled stately plump Buck Mulligan but felt no charity for the Parisian bums, the clochards. Sally and Toni became the lovely seaside girls and Paris seemed pleased to offer her ineluctable modality. I went to Chartres to see the cathedral that Soutine had painted, *"à quelle heure part le train pour Chartres?"* A grey tour in the drizzle of Chartres, an expensive meal and back to Paris to polish our eyes at the Orangerie drinking in Cezanne, Gauguin and the raiment of impressionist colours. Sally finally decided to go to London. At the train station she begged me to come with her. I couldn't. I wanted to return to Spain to do my lithos. There was no real love between us, she was just beginning to blossom as a woman. I told her Nietzsche had his cat for company, and I had my projects to begin. It was my attempt at being gentle.

When I returned to Madrid, Paco Baron the sculptor and now my close friend put me in touch with Dimitri Papageorgiou, an affable Greek lithographer who had a small studio on Modesto Lafuente, a working class area. Dimitri was enthusiastic about doing a suite with me as such a project was unusual. Most artists came to him to do one or two prints. Recently Manolo Millares' wife had done a suite. This connection made me feel a part of the art scene in Madrid, a project that had scope. Dimitri's press was an old hand-operated affair that added to the authentic flavour of the project, made it seem romantic. To further imbue myself in Joyce and the past I rented a small room in the centre of town where I could pore over his novel and make drawings outlining my ideas for my first prints. I happened to see an article in a Spanish magazine on the Feria in Seville, a festivity Joyce wrote about that I had missed on my excursion south. I combined this with a photo of Joyce I'd seen in *Time* magazine and a sense of the Andalusian landscape I had travelled, adding touches of my own life on Thornton Avenue in Venice, California. A period of time, akin to Joyce's residency at the tower, where he too had set himself to the side of life's mainstream. This collage of images I hoped would suggest the montage effect of his novel.

As winter began to set in, I was offered a job with Phil Yordan. Mr Yordan, who reminded me of Mr Magoo, was in the beginning stages of preparing a production of *The Royal Hunt of the Sun*. He wanted me to fashion several large heads in bronze for their production. Irving Lerner, who directed the film, wanted me to act in it. He thought I could play the part of Atahualpa, the Indian King who is overthrown by the Conquistadors. Phil didn't take this idea seriously. He was familiar with my sculpture since he had commissioned a head of his wife, Faith. Maybe the moment was too informal. Context and presentation may have given me a chance but it would be a long shot. What was curious was that an actor that I had worked with in a play at Bard College was there to read for the part that Christopher Plummer would eventually play. Phil was not familiar with my acting. When I read for the part at Irving's request, Phil dismissed it. This job would finance my lithography project, a happy serendipity, which I was delighted to take advantage of. I set to work doing research for Phil. We settled on the idea of using three Inca heads as the subjects. I would copy them for the film. The originals were ceramic pots, portrait heads with the combined function of being vessels. The naturalistic expressions seemed of actual people. I enlarged these portraits several times and did away with the functional aspects to create large, imposing images that would be cast in bronze, polished to resemble gold.

I should tell you that I didn't much care for this job. I didn't do it for the money as I didn't realise I would be so well paid. I did it because I felt that I was expected to get a job. In a way it is OK not to worry about money or whether or not a project will be a success. That is a specific goal unlike when I'm working for myself speculating on the direction of a particular painting. Painting because I'm enthralled with the idea of my own intuitive invention good or bad, I feel I'm working for myself. I wanted to bring this in before I slip in another incident.

I had been on a beautiful island and I was doing portrait heads of famous actors while they rested between the filming. My parents were there as well and there was a great deal of scurrying around which can be enjoyable in a beautiful environment. The point I'm making has to do with a quality of feeling alive, of living with all of your faculties tingling. Everyone needs to feel excited about their work, in short how they spend their time. That it is one of the real challenges in the art of living. Sometimes we are gifted with an experience which reminds us of this epiphany, this excitation.

One morning I was taken for a ride on the back of a motor scooter down a narrow road with no traffic. We were going ten miles an hour just floating above the ground. On each side of the road were olive tree orchards. Some of the trees were said to be two thousand years old. Their branches extended into a blue sky in gestures which reminded me of the movements made by modern dancers. I was in Majorca, on the road near the village of Deia, but I felt exhilarated as if I were moving in time either back to a mythological period or that plain in reality where one experiences the presence of history and time like the branches of these trees reaching out in an eternal present. I like the way Henry Miller explained this feeling when he talks about the light in Greece and how standing where Agamemnon once stood he thought he could feel his presence as well. Well, I wanted to slip in this small moment, this moment of pure pleasure, this luna park ride—as looking at the drama of these trees was one of the most beautiful experiences of my life. To think that they will be dancing after I'm gone, or that other people may be equally touched by this landscape seems important, more important than working for wages. I needed to tell you this just now as I was working on something which wasn't so exciting for me and I wanted to show you a contrasting moment so you could perhaps feel inspired. I believe this plateau is visited by people from time to time. When an idea gets taken up again and pushed forward the idea lives on, maybe this is reincarnation. From this plateau, this arena of feelings, I envisage mankind could go anywhere and survive on very essential basics. It starts with a simple ride on the back of a scooter and ends with the achievement of world peace or a piece of art. The accelerator of a new psychic reality. Of course if I'm a monster, we are all in for hell.

The three heads that I translated into bronze took several months to complete. They were worked on at a leisurely pace at my studio, which I now shared with Peter, a painter who kept me entertained with stories and in touch with what was happening on the scene. As I worked Peter kept talking of a trip to Morocco. I was very conscientious about working on the sculptures, which were finally used in the opening montages to offset the credits, and also in a dream sequence that occurred later in the film. By the time the commission was completed (for which I was very well compensated), Peter's wanderlust had totally infected me. Having finished my work for Phil Yordan I thought I'd give myself a breather before returning to work on my litho project. The allure of Morocco can be intoxicating as it is so close to Spain, one can almost see the coast of Africa from Algeciras.

20

Beauty And Genius

"Hello Mr Bowles?"

"Yes."

I introduced myself and was invited to visit at tea time around three. I didn't bring Peter along. Paul Bowles gave me his address, explaining that most taxi drivers would know where he lived. I was driven out away from Tangiers up into a hill amid a collection of small villas and apartment buildings. It was quiet there except for the rattling of the cicadas. A breeze came up. Mr Bowles answered the door.

"Come in, I believe a friend of yours is upstairs."

Ascending the stairs I felt an orderly presence, a pleasant conciseness to Mr Bowles. I felt exhilarated to meet him, his blue eyes made no special demands. Behind the door he opened was a neat sunny library and standing at a window was a figure holding a large photo album. The slight figure, dressed in dark denim turned to face me.

The beautiful face framed in long hair was not familiar to me immediately. Rather a sense of the fate of beauty came to mind; in a flash I saw myself destroying the beauty so that I could hold it, possess it in memory as something which belonged to me.

"For God's sake! Jim?"

Morrison's smile broke my train of thought and a delicious explosion of recognition erased a dark truth. I turned briefly to acknowledge Bowles as Jim put down the book, the tension broken.

"Howdy pal, what'ya do'n in Morocco?"

I stood speechless as Jim approached. He was so beautiful.

"Yippie," I found myself saying, which I thought was rather insipid, and Jim put his arms around my shoulders."Have I changed that much?" he kidded.

But in fact he had worked rather hard at making himself beautiful. He was his own artwork. He was a masterpiece. His beauty radiated intelligence as well as a physical magnetism. And it was daunting to see, to be near, to know that someone could be that beautiful, perfection realised. There was the feel of some delicate quality, masculine to be sure, a gentle presence, beautiful to the extent that I wanted to offer gifts, to present a reward. Maybe you could say it was love. It was the way I felt looking at beauty, at the Venus de Milo, at a nude by Titian or Modigliani. But it was Jim.

Paul nudged the moment.

"We were just about to have a bowl of kif."

Extending his arm he indicated the sitting area around a small table, under a shelf of books.

"Jim was showing me his newly published folio of poems."

"Wow! Gees Jim, I'm sure pleased for you."

"Not the least bit envious, Michael?" Bowles inquired cheerfully.

I laughed, embarrassed by the truth of my jealousy. I was envious of Jim's beauty, but I could also admire it as I could his poems. His world was dark, and there was an unpleasant sense of foreboding—

something reptilian there. In grade school, I had gone out one afternoon with a friend to the Los Angeles riverbed: sandy gravel and silence. There was a horned toad on a small mound with his head held high and a horrible sense that I had been there as well, a moment in my life in a past incarnation before finally seeing reality as a person. This sense of the history of consciousness also came through what Jim wrote about, being a voyeur and a witness to the cruelty of humanity. I didn't want to face cruelty so I would make a world of cheerfulness, of bright colours, of Italian gestures, of sensual pleasures, in the sunlight where there were no shadows.

"Jesus, Jim, I'm really pleased for you."

Jim's expression remained pensive. He was enjoying the moment. Bowles' own work was close to Jim's vision. Both scrutinized reality. Jim hadn't come to Bowles for approval, but as a gesture or a need to be near a kindred spirit.

A man in white burnoose came into the room. His flowing movements settled my excitement. The metal tray he placed on the small table between us contained a bowl of kif and three small pipes, clay pipes with long wooden stems. My eyes automatically followed the white gown and came to rest on a framed photo hanging opposite me. It was a photo of the desert in which the demarcations of strata had various textures, but no visible sky, it created a claustrophobic and hypnotic effect. Bowles noticed my interest.

"The photographer fell to his death. He had stepped back to get a fuller view and misjudged his footing. I miss his enthusiasm."

We both looked at Paul to share a moment of silence for his lost friend. Bowles handed me a pipe, which he was now lighting with a match. He did the same for Jim and himself. The kif took effect instantly. The silence between us felt like a solid mass... my mind began to race.

"Jim, let me look at your book." Bowles handed me the volume. Holding something in my hand felt reassuring. I wasn't in any danger, the kif was merely overstimulating. Jim let out a large puff of smoke.

"Kind of neat that we're here. When you called Paul I told him of our breakfast with your mom, and the play she had written after smoking kif. Paul's never read it. He has given me his novel, *The Sheltering Sky*."

"There are a thousand questions I'll have for both of you when I leave, curious delay of thinking!" I said trying to be clever, "I hope I think of one now."

"Do either of you want to buy an island in Malaysia?" Paul asked returning to things more down to earth. "I won't be going back there, so I offer it to whomever comes through. One never knows..."

"Malaysia, eh, hum," Jim mused.

I didn't speculate, it was difficult to focus.

"Nah, I think I'll stay close to Paris. I like the history of the poets who lived there. There is a there, there, and not much anywhere else." Jim was making a reference to Gertrude Stein's comment; 'there's no there, there'.

"I knew Miss Stein, she asked me to look after her poodle. The dog had an affection for my pant legs. I had come to inquire about a poem I had given her of mine to read. She felt my metaphor was not actual, that it had nothing to do with the reality of my poem, the experience. I rewrote it and also followed her advice coming to Morocco. I was mostly composing then, but I wanted to write."

Jim and I were enjoying hearing about this period so different than our own, which had no centre for us. Paris was the magic cauldron.

"I studied for a time with Aaron Copland. I mix things together. My music is impressionistic, impressions of everything alive musically, that is, incorporating many influences. Folk music is especially invigorating. Let me play something for you."

Paul got up and deftly placed a 45 disc on his machine.

"This is a Berber tune, recently recorded."

The kif by then had cleared my head, and the sound was crystalline and sweet. A guitar and a flute chopped into each other giving a cubist feel to the sound, not unlike Paul's own compositions. The feel was unpredictable, which is a kind of magic. Jim sat very still. Bowles also sat frozen, listening. My eyes returned to the strange photo of the desert hanging in front of me; there was no life in it, no blade of grass, only texture upon texture, emptiness, a wanting. I had been there before. A place where I was alone. Each visit to the land of high had its own continuity, a welcome sense of familiarity. As if I were returning to where we had left off, me and being high. I could return to the desert in Palm Springs, or the seashore in Venice. Return to a zone inside the time/space continuum and being inside the eternal now, I was alive in all time and space. Sitting quietly looking at this empty photo of strata, layer upon layer, forever immobile, it occurred to me that that was why Jim never feared death. He had visited life eternal on LSD. Everything was glued together, life-death, space-time. Reality was all one.

The clean smell of Paul's jellaba brought my thoughts back into the room.

Jim had a vague smile on his face, he had picked up on my revelation. His smile suggested he had a special travelling permit to eternity. Death, his old friend, had no dominion and was kept waiting.

When the music stopped, silence held the space for a moment.

"Paul, that was outstanding! Too bad Manzarek isn't here with us; he'd dig the rhythms. Ah, it must have been stimulating to have been around all of the geniuses you've known," Jim probed.

"If I talk about myself," Paul spoke slowly, lending weight to his thoughts without pretension, "if I do that... then I'll have to exist. But the joke is temporary, each of us must face death. What happens in our lives is always unexpected, you know. The word 'genius' has no actual meaning for me. We are rather, planets. Planets circling in space, never really touching. Romance is a Hollywood illusion. Sometimes, the planets brush up against each other and for a time there is company. That is genius, or genius is a need for company... it amounts to the same thing. Finally, however, we have to be self-sufficient. That is why I love the desert. It mirrors our aloneness. It is vast, the eye travels to a finite place, the horizon. What we fill this space with amounts to our genius to amuse ourselves, it's a game."

"Yeah, ah hah." Jim would take a stab at the question of genius.

"Moving reality around, putting it together for yourself."

After a pause, Bowles continued, "Yes, intelligence mixed with passion. We need a centre, a focal point, something to do. I have left a marker. Another artist might take a similar road, never the same one but somehow related, in sympathy."

There was a pause again.

"Capote and Williams I think have been trapped by America. I feel lucky to have gotten out, away from the materialism. Recognition is also a poison. Appreciation at a distance is another relationship. The need for fame eventually empties you out. The fame... the need consumes you. But you know that, right, Michael?"

"Yeah, that's Hollywood. But you know I hadn't realised, it's a disease that affects all of the arts. I guess I thought they were purer."

"You remind me of your father," Paul said, but I didn't understand what he meant by that.

"Huh ha," Jim added. "You have lived in Morocco for so long. Why?"

Jim shifted his body.

"It's a beautiful canvas, mysterious by nature, unknowable even. It is an empty canvas where I can place people, watch them struggle against the vastness. The desert and the sky. And the sky protects them, it holds them, it separates them from the endless blackness of space. The elements are simple. A pot of tea, mint leaves in hot water made on a charcoal brazier." Paul paused and gave us a grin.

"The textures of people become more defined, even desperate, but defined by being reduced to the naked truths of their needs and fears."

I felt the essence of what aloneness was for Bowles, which had its own unique wonderment or pleasure for life. There was his delight to reason with his mind. And he had his wife Jane. They were mirrors for each other's thoughts. They had company. She was ill then.

"Please give our respects to your wife," Jim said as if he had read my mind. I was ready to go as well. I'd be travelling to Marrakech the next day.

"Where should I stay in Marrakech?"

"Hotel Central."

Mr Bowles walked us downstairs to get the taxi he had called. I felt Paul was sad our visit had been so brief, but he understood we'd have some of our own schmoozing to do. Jim gripped his copy of *The Sheltering Sky* and I knew we'd be going our separate ways. No wild nights. The kif had unsettled us, odd considering what we had lived through only a few years back in LA. It was OK. We had seen each other and we both looked well reflected in each other's eyes. Why spoil a beautiful picture with too much shading?

"See ya," I said, leaving Jim to the taxi. I descended into the Kasbah and headed for my hotel. It had already been a full day and another full one would follow.

21

Endless Bazaar

Thinking about my visit with Bowles and Jim in Tangiers and about the kif which we smoked from a clay bowl that was the custom, I had mused, 'Paul Bowles—clay bowls'. This wasn't meant to be disrespectful, just a summing up. Peter reported this to a writer he had fallen in with who asked me if he could use this quip in a novel he was writing. I wasn't that attached to my pun so I consented. I did not discuss Paul Bowles with them. This so-called novelist weighed his own thoughts on a scale with diamonds, sitting cross-legged in jodhpurs looking very colonial in his rented villa in the French sector of town. It was much more respectable than the native quarters where we lodged. The novelist was basing his epic on stories he had heard about a legendary character that the natives had nicknamed

Steve Maxitone. Maxitone was a form of speed that had entirely overtaken this fellow. He set up residence in a cave mysteriously located deep in the bowels of the earth. It was no longer known what alchemical projects this chap was up to, but whatever they were, they were of no interest to me. I was almost off drugs. Kif unnerved me. The whole business of drugs at this point was upsetting. I didn't much like this novelist, a pretentious character all round. I excused myself to return to my hotel or go browse about. Morocco was a high all by itself.

The weather in December in Marrakech is fresh and warm during the day and chilly at night. At the town square known as the Al Jamaa Fna or 'place of rebirth', scores of colourful people gather to examine the maze of wares and stalls scattered in front of the covered bazaar. The bazaar is an endless labyrinth. In this open plaza you can buy food and drink and have your fortune told by a method combining pieces of ocean-worn glass, coins, dice, and cards. This is employed by a bright-eyed man with a straggly beard who seems more Chinese than Moroccan. After careful deliberation over these sacred objects and the solicitous examination of his client, your future boils down to a good holiday. The festive atmosphere is also graced by the presence of male dancers who jump rhythmically in their black and white outfits to a mesmerising beat of a chorus of kettledrums. It is the plaza where talents are proudly displayed even if they are merely the private ceremonies of a man praying in front of a makeshift altar. This can be an arrangement of flowers, mirrors, candles, cards, oranges and feathers laid out over a prayer rug balanced in a delicate array of magical construction.

It is here where two Mongoloid idiots are placed out for a bit of warm afternoon sun. If the personality of the Moroccan seems elusive, hidden, or strange, clothed in jelabas, like hooded thoughts going about their business, that impression eventually gives way to a clear feeling of communication. In the Jamaa Fna all is understood, all is clear. Looking at a dancer and admiring his lace shirt, I thought it would be nice to have one. When the dancer finished his dance he offered me his shirt. If one felt thirsty, magically the waterman was there, offering a drink. Away from sophisticated technologies, these people seemed to understand simple desires more directly, since simple desires are not masked in reticence. Energy flows there... the currents filling the air. It was not hysteria or manic excitement, it's the real intuitive centres unclogged by the pollution of protocol in modern society. It is a kind of energy and openness that seems overbearing in its blatant nakedness, an energy you might like to enjoy somewhat at a distance at first. A distance that can allow for acclimatisation. The teahouses, small terraces that overlook the Jamaa Fna, are where European visitors rendezvous and cool out from the dazzle of this circus.

Having taken a shave, I felt refreshed and gazing toward the setting sun I saw a beautiful female leaving as Peter appeared, bubbling over about a party he wanted me to go to. Without missing a beat I grabbed Peter and hustled out after the figure that was so spellbinding. She disappeared in the confusion of the twilight crowd. Peter thought I had exaggerated her beauty, which I talked about as he guided me to the party. He hadn't noticed her at all, which I thought was strange. Upstairs, above a small courtyard, a group of young travellers were speaking gaily in different languages. The brightly lit room was literally packed to the gills and I didn't feel like pushing my way in; I was still thinking of the beautiful woman I had just seen. I happened to glance down into the dimly lit courtyard and I thought that I saw two people surreptitiously carrying a body. Quietly, I descended to check out my observations. A man and a woman were carrying a limp form wrapped in a blanket. It was hard for them to deal with opening the door while holding the figure. "What has happened, can I help?" The man stared at me, trying to push me away with his eyes. He blurted, "overdosed." Entering, they placed the figure on a cot opening the blanket, letting the body breathe. I stood there, stunned, looking at a white naked figure of a young woman. I was not sure it wasn't the woman that had so captured my heart earlier at the teahouse. "Get away, go away," cried the voice of the man fiercely attacking me. "Are you sure she will be alright?" I droned back, "Yes. Yes. Yes." The words hit me like bullets but they were not reassuring. Peter or someone upstairs could better appraise the situation, I thought, and I bolted up the stairs and through the crowd to find him.

Peter was pleasantly engaged in conversation but he could see I was upset. "Come downstairs, someone is dying, it may be that girl I saw at the teahouse." "What?" "Yes, hurry, I think it's serious." Peter was a bit reluctant but he left quickly. Downstairs, the door had been closed. I just opened it. The figure of the woman seemed to show no signs of life. The man and woman were conferring off to the side. The man was visibly shaken. Turning, he saw Peter and me standing in the doorway and began shouting at us, instructing us to leave, frantically reassuring us she would be okay. Her bleached face was slightly contorted, Peter was pulling at my arm. It was impossible to discern absolutely if this was the woman that so appealed to me. The man drew a knife and began approaching us, yelling "Get out, get out!" Peter jerked me away. I snapped to at the sight of the knife, and we ran. I don't know why we didn't go to the police. I think we just lost sight of the fact that there were police to go to. Early the following morning we made several inquiries about the European with the Van Dyke beard and the drug incident. Apparently someone had alerted the police, but they eluded them. The girl had been lucky; she had lived.

This put us somewhat at ease. Nevertheless, having been in Marrakech we thought this might be a good moment to go elsewhere lest we fall into some other high-calibre intrigue. On the recommendation of a Dutch couple, we decided to take the daylong ride to Essaouira, a seacoast town due west of Marrakech. I'm sure I would have been deeply upset no matter who had overdosed. I was afraid of heroin and never went in that direction. It is curiously sad, in another way, how quickly we move on. I was guilty as well of treating life as an entertainment, but I hadn't realised it. By late afternoon we arrived feeling pleasant and anxious to explore the white sparkling village dressed in blue trim. Coming down the road that led to this tiny village we could see the Atlantic stretching to the horizon. As the bus came to a stop in the town square a man who introduced himself as the Mayor greeted us. He immediately invited us to join him for a smoke of his personal kif. I didn't wish to embarrass the Mayor by making a big issue of smoking. We sat down at a small, round table and as he chatted with us in clipped English, we watched him deftly chopping and blending the leaves of kif in a rhythmic flow. Women dressed in clean white robes walked by us. The robes were slit along the side and through these white curtains fluorescent undergarments of the most electric gender added a shocking touch to the placid white charm of our environment.

After a brief chat we excused ourselves and took our leave to find a hotel room. Essaouira seemed like a ghost town. There was no one else staying at the hotel. We rented a large, spacious room and decided to go out exploring. Along a parapet of cobblestones lined by workshops illuminated by single electric bulbs we breathed in the thick soggy air filled with moisture from the ocean. Unable to find a restaurant we returned to our hotel for sleep. The moisture was so thick that the sheets were wet. Lying in bed body heat quickly overcame the damp.

We were up bright and early. I had brought my Moroccan dyes and some paper along with the idea of doing some watercolours. I had gone to great lengths to get these dyes through a Moroccan painter who had befriended me in Marrakech. So far I hadn't had a chance to use them. The sky was a transparent blue. The air fresh and salty. Amidst groupings of tiny buildings that made up Essaouira we saw a young girl hanging up colourful laundry in front of her bungalow.

She was Dutch and Peter was giving it his all. I drifted off with paints under my arm. I met a young couple who were on their honeymoon staying with a Moroccan family near the beach. They invited me for lunch and afterwards I headed up the road that led away from Essaouira hoping for a dramatic vista that might inspire a watercolour. Below me on a vast expanse of sand a man was shepherding two camels. The camels seemed to be leading the man. No sooner would he catch up with one of the dromedaries when the second would head out in a diagonal direction. The man ran in zigzags between the two camels who had the upper hand. This brought to mind a Moroccan saying, shedding new light on its meaning: *'a bowl of kif in the morning gives the strength in the afternoon of a hundred camels in the courtyard'*. It took a great deal of hassling to guide camels from one place to another. Paul Bowles had used this saying as a title for one of his books, *A Hundred Camels in the Courtyard*. I sent Bowles a letter thanking him for his hospitality and briefly recounting some of our adventures. I decorated the envelope with the dye colours that I bought in Marrakech, which proved to be quite rich. Peter and I stayed on a day longer and I managed to paint a few pictures. The best I gave to Peter's pretty young Dutch girl as she was delighted with the colours. Back in Marrakech Peter and I had another adventure involving a European lady who was down on her luck. I don't remember her name, but I remember the strong sense of pity that I felt for her. When first we saw her, she was standing in front of a food stall demanding food. The Moroccans were laughing at her. She was carrying on like a banshee. She said that they wouldn't feed her. She had been living on no money for quite some time and it was not unusual for Moroccans to feed the poor gratis. A stranded European seemed to tickle their sense of power. Peter and I decided that we had better bring her back to Europe before it was too late. Her manner was angry and she had not bathed in quite a while. She resisted the idea of going back with us. We reassured her we had only her best interests in mind and that we would pay her way, that we wanted nothing in return. Almost miraculously she seemed to readjust to a level of civilization that included eating with utensils and combing her hair. She became almost polite by the time we put her on the train to Amsterdam in Madrid.

22

Plumtree's Potted Meat

What a relief to be home in grey Madrid. It would suffice to visit Café Gijón and listen to Carlos Arossa chant a poem or insist on my buying a pair of antique glasses. When Peter left town I decided it was time for me to get back to my Joyce series of lithographs. After all, why had I knocked myself out working for Philip Yordan? Certainly not to be a tour guide for bizarre trips to Morocco! It was time to do some work for myself. Dimitri was pleased to see me and it was a good moment to set to work on a series of prints. No one else was working with him at that time. His studio was tiny and his supply of stones limited. As we pulled the prints Dimitri reground the stones to keep me supplied with fresh surfaces. I was enthralled with the process; I grilled Dimitri for information around the corner from his studio over a glass of wine and chorizo. Some of the prints required more ink and others less. Once I scraped the stone during the actual printing adding more light to the image. I was using Joyce's novel as a springboard for an impressionistic excursion to the places I had been visiting in Europe; vistas, cafés, hotel rooms, any locale that I felt reflected the sensations his novel had evoked. The style of the images began to reflect a kind of Pop Art view of Bonnard, van Dongen and Lautrec. This seemed appropriate enough to the period of the novel. I was mixing Joyce with these impressionists and exploring a new medium, having a good time all around.

   I worked with Dimitri as often as he could be at his studio. He hired a printer and I hungrily watched every print that came off the press. The press was hand operated, tricky but charming. This collection of images eventually numbered about twenty different scenes. The prints were pulled in editions of varying numbers, some images were terminated at twenty-five copies and others stopped at sixty. Altogether we created a pile of about six hundred prints. I had portfolios made so people could acquire a suite and have a place for safekeeping. Along with the lithos I produced four small cut-out figurines to accompany the portfolio of graphics. Joyce, Molly Bloom, a 'seaside girl' holding an umbrella and Blazes Boylan. They stood about ten inches high. On the backside of these figures I quoted several Joycean phrases that had amused me and that pertained to Joyce's characters. For Joyce I wrote: 'signatures of all things I am here to read'. Molly received: 'yes, I will, yes'. Naturally, the seaside girl got: 'those girls, those lovely seaside girls'. Only Bloom went blank but Blazes got: 'the salute of Almidano Artifoni's sturdy trousers swallowed by a closing door'. These pieces were miraculously cast at Codina using a sand mould rather than the lost wax technique; they were so good at it. You could not tell the difference after the bronze had been patinaed.

On March 22, 1968 my first one-man show opened at Galeria Seiquer. The gallery was a small room which featured print shows and it was located at 3 Santa Catalina, across the street from the prestigious Academy of Fine Arts. I came early and was greeted by a fellow who interviewed me for Irish radio. In a whirlwind tour around the gallery he asked me if it were not so that this image had come from such and such a sequence in the book. He was much more of an authority on *Ulysses* than myself and really only wanted my confirmation about his observations, which I was happy to supply as the gallery began to fill up. The announcement which the gallery had sent out featured a photo of Pablo Serrano, a very well-known sculptor, with one arm around me and the other outstretched gesturing in welcome. My dad had the idea for this sort of announcement. Many of Serrano's patrons came to see the show and bought prints. My father, who had watched the process of my working, had offered advice on certain images as well.

Gail Getty, who came with my father, bought an entire suite and they left me to deal with the numerous questions that people seemed to want to ask. One lady journalist wanted to interview me privately over lunch the following day. She was very taken with the composition of one of the prints in which the perspective had been split: a sky filled with floating images appearing behind a faceless man sitting at a table and a woman with features recumbent on a bed. Below the image Joyce is quoted: 'What is home without Plumtree's Potted Meat? Incomplete! With it an abode of Bliss.' She felt sure that I had borrowed my composition from El Greco's *The Burial of Count Orgaz*, a mural he had painted in a chapel in Toledo, adjacent to the home of Simon Levy, who had been his patron. This was a flattering thought, but not from my mind. No doubt she was looking for some sexual attention. How could I disappoint her twice?

The lithos were all single-colour affairs, mostly black and white. This, along with the fact that Joyce's work, being anti-Catholic, was not held in high regard in Spain, limited my sales. Dad suggested that I colour the prints. The task seemed overwhelming. Dimitri thought perhaps he could help me distribute some of them to hotels, which often had been his patrons. At that moment all I felt like doing was sitting in Café Gijón to recuperate, re-evaluate. I placed several copies of a litho featuring a green figure of Joyce brandishing a cane and announcing in Spanish my show with a paraphrase of Joyce that proved with algebra that Michael Lawrence was Shakespeare. These I 'modestly' hung in all my favourite haunts, which I frequented expecting to be hailed as the new Lautrec. It was fun pretending to be back at the turn of the century. Alas, no one recognised me or this litho's resemblance to Lautrec's image of Aristide Bruant. I tried to stay cheerful but the let-down I felt was drastic. All of the energy and time I'd put into this project and the money stood facing me, deflating my hopes. It was the wrong project for a Spanish audience… I should have done Don Quixote. Or I could have taken my project to Dublin. But I didn't think of these things then. I didn't have a stage manager, an agent to guide me.

One night I went into the Red Lion, a small bar, downstairs from my apartment on Hurtado de Mendoza. It catered to an English clientele; there was a lot of beer drinking and darts. Sitting in the corner was a dark haired woman whom I hadn't seen before. I introduced myself and began explaining who I was and about my show, would she like to see it? The lady's name was Isabella. Although she didn't seem too impressed with my opening remarks she agreed to meet me at the gallery the next day. I thought she was rather striking, even mysterious, and had a most pleasant voice. At the gallery she seemed much more alive than at our meeting the night before. She was delighted by the lithographs, as she thought one image resembled her, and was herself being charming. I was delighted with her reaction and taken with her manner. I felt that I was making a new friend. She was an engaging conversationalist. I hungrily followed her flow of stories which captured my attention. Listening to Isabella talking about her life in New York and her friends, I felt as if I were back in that noisy, smelly, exciting hustle-bustle. I walked her home, enthralled by her plans and dreams. As we stood under the streetlight waiting for the portero to let her inside, I fantasised about spending time with Isabella. We agreed to meet the next evening for dinner and we would go hear some flamenco singers, something that she had always wanted to do, something I had never done. I hustled back to my apartment feeling that flush of excitement, that sense of being alive which tells you that you are infatuated. Finally, maybe my dream had come true. Here was a mature woman.

I thought of this night as the beginning of our romance. I chose an environment filled with energy, an informal place known as The Caves. It is a touristic restaurant but also a lot of fun; a subterranean pirates' cave where wrought iron chandeliers hang over wooden benches shared by all the patrons. The house specialty is the open fire cooking of rabbit and the minstrels who walk around playing guitars and singing. The student laughter and wine add to the erotic 17th century replay. We quickly gave into the atmosphere, allowing ourselves to be swept away along with everybody else. From there we went to a club to see flamenco dancers wailing and clacking, beating their hearts out expressing the pathos of love. The ambiance of both places permitted us time to observe each other without much conversation. I was having a good time eyeing the dancers who were having a good time with me. Isabella didn't approve of my reactions, which I felt were innocent; after all, I wasn't going to leave with the dancer, I was just showing off. Apparently this exchange of attentions between myself and the dancers had disturbed Isabella;

she wanted to go home early. I was surprised at this and apologized. She said it was nothing, but she couldn't help the way she felt, maybe she'd see me tomorrow. I'd have to be more delicate with her feelings. Being away from the swing of things I was totally unaware that, in a way, she was putting the make on me too. Her feigning jealousy made my attentions to the dancers more important than they had actually been. She was telling me in a roundabout way that she cared. I called her the next afternoon to tell her that my father wasn't going to be at home that night, and we could have a quiet candlelit dinner. She reminded me of Sandra, whom I adored in high school, I'd never scored with her, being that I never complied with her request that I get a driver's licence first. I'd have to be more attentive to Isabella's needs, I'd have to be on my toes, so to speak.

Opening the door I gave her a light kiss on the cheek and a brief tour of the apartment.

"How delightful everything looks. And candles, how romantic."

"Hungry?"

"Famished."

I wasn't wearing my glasses. The candlelight softened Isabella's appearance. In my dream world her voice suggested every vision of a beautiful woman that I could ever have wished for. Each movement was under close scrutiny and had its hypnotic effect.

Isabella was smiling. It was a sly smile.

"The beauty of anything is in its style."

We were flirting in our heads, not with our words.

"Yes, yes, yes." I fell under her spell.

"Michael, stop being a tempest. Let it come slowly. Would your mother approve of your getting involved with an older woman?"

"We won't tell her; it will be our secret."

"This wine is delicious."

"Ten cents a bottle."

"Really, it's unbelievable."

"You're avoiding my question." Were we going to make love was clearly written on my face.

"No I'm not. I'm taking my time."

"What is your favourite museum?" I thought that that was neutral ground. She didn't seem to want to respond to my previous question.

"When I was a little girl, I used to go to the Metropolitan Museum. I loved doing my homework in the Egyptian Temple. It was so quiet there and away from the boys who chased me at school."

I had just been thinking that she looked Egyptian. "How old were you when the boys started chasing after you?"

"I was seven. They wanted me to lift my skirt for them. I did and after that they never let me alone."

"I bet you liked the idea."

"Later. At seven I was interested in books. I began to read when I was five."

"Well, you beat me there."

"What were you doing at seven?"

"I was learning to ride my bike."

"That's precocity," she teased.

"Do you remember the first book that you ever read?"

"Dostoyevsky's *Notes from Underground*."

"That's precious!" We laughed. I was wondering how I was going to bridge the jump into the sack.

"Don't you want to make love to me?" Isabella offered.

"Yes." I came around the table and held her head in my hands, kissing her on the mouth.

"Let me take a bath first. Go wait in the bedroom."

I kissed her again and headed for the bedroom. I got undressed and lay under the covers. I felt ridiculous. I got up, threw on a robe and went to the bathroom. "Hello in there. How's it coming?"

"Fine. I'll be right out!"

"C'mon, let me in. It's no fun out here. I'm coming in."

Isabella was laughing as I went in. She was out of the tub with a towel wrapped around her.

"You cheated," I accused.

"Which way to the bedroom?"

"Follow me."

We walked arm in arm to the bedroom.

"The lighting is too strong. Don't you have any candles?"

"I'll be right back."

When I returned the lights were out and Isabella was under the covers. "Put the candles over here."

Her body was round and firm. I kissed her hungrily. Isabella stopped me.

"Softly! Hold both of my lips between yours and then kiss me full on the mouth. Don't be impatient; everything lovely comes slowly." Her voice was warm.

I took her lower lip and kissed it: the flesh in my mouth was like a persimmon.

My tongue felt her teeth.

"Slower, Michael."

When I kissed her on the mouth between her lips she sank her tongue deep into my mouth. Her hand on my penis was more than I could take.

"No, no, too fast."

I had come. I had wanted to be inside of her. She had changed that. She reached for a cigarette.

"I'm sorry, Isabella."

She lit her cigarette and looked away.

"It's not that fast for a woman."

"Teach me."

She was getting out of bed.

"Teach me, please!"

Isabella was dressing. I started to climb out of bed.

"Don't bother. I'll show myself out."

I got out of bed and went over to her.

"Don't Michael. Don't see me out."

I stood awkwardly, watching her lace up her boots. I watched helplessly as she left the bedroom. I heard the front door close.

The following night she explained to me some of the facts of life that she thought had eluded my sex education. Isabella calmly told me that a woman has a little penis called a clitoris, that's located above the vagina and that by rubbing it or licking it she could be aroused to really enjoy sex, that she would 'come' too. Her treatment of the subject I thought was clinical, not what I had expected to ensue from the passions I felt. She said that I shouldn't worry about it, coming too soon. She'd show me the next time we went to bed. My feelings settled. She asked me if I wanted to go to Morocco with her as her travelling companion. Of course I did. She was pleased with my answer and held out her hand for mine. Isabella was older than myself, I guessed thirty-two or three. Who knows, maybe in time she would feel the way I felt toward her. She liked me but I was the one who was passionate. I didn't want to lose her. So I'd put up with another excursion to Morocco.

23

Shuttlecock

It is spring in Tangiers. We are both fascinated, sitting in the Suco Chico, that small plaza, thirty feet wide, lined by coffeehouses that face each other. Everyone stops there for their first cup of tea. The sounds of music blend and mix like the people themselves, some in robes, some wearing European dress: tourists and hustlers all moving up or down the hill creating a dazzling arena. The radios are playing Elvis and the Beatles in the Suco Chico. An English bloke is saying 'tincture of cannabis', it strikes me as a good title for something. We are sipping mint tea. A redheaded Moroccan has just come up to the table and is fast-talking us about a party he gave for William S. Burroughs while ripping apart a local comic book, pure William S., eh, pure mimicry, pure mirror. Isabella is delighted by the attention and the circus of activity. I am pleased that she is. Isabella and I were held captive. It was a sight I had experienced before but the magic of it never fails to be hypnotic. Soon we were joined by another young hustler who wanted us to come with him. We didn't like the way he tried to push aside the redheaded one, whom we had found charming. We begged off and said we were leaving, we'd see him later. The redheaded fellow left, but the other guy just kept going at us, even as we left the café heading up the road to find a hotel away from the activity of Suco Chico. I said that I had been to Tangiers before and that it was not necessary for him to accompany us any further. He threw his arms up in the air, and shouted a few words we didn't need to have translated. I explained to Isabella that I thought it was a bad idea for us to get too friendly with these guys; they never let you off the hook. She thought I was exaggerating. I said nothing.

We found a hotel at the top of the quarter and checked in for a nap. I was anxious to continue with my sexual education, she was in need of rest. The wolfen cry of the muezzin awoke us. We went out to see Tangiers at night. We continued up the road leading toward the European section. At the top of the road was a small square filled by stalls with canvas roofs, but the stalls were all closing. There were a few cars there as the road was wide enough; in the Medina there was only foot traffic. We sat at a café and ordered some food. A man sat down and began talking with us. He was middle-aged, pleasant and spoke good English. The gist of his story was that the world had gotten too complicated, people could no longer trust each other. The best life was a simple one. Certainly you couldn't argue with that. Isabella drew him out and made her own comments, talking about the lack of social justice and how she had protested against the war and had been driven back by tear gas in Washington. I was beginning to feel uneasy about all this candour. It was one thing for her to be so open with me and quite another to express herself so freely at night sitting alone atop the Suco Chico, no buffers. I felt uneasy. I announced to her that I had a headache and suggested that she should come back with me to the hotel. She was happy chatting away with this perfect stranger. Where was her common sense? There was nothing menacing about him, but then who knows what his motives were? Perhaps he just wanted to chat, but I sat there getting more uptight. I think my squirming eventually got to the stranger who took his leave.

"What in the world is wrong with you, Michael?" Isabella asked in the most pleasant of tones. I was in a cold sweat. It was nothing, there was no reason for my being paranoid. I had no excuse. I had never told her of my previous experiences in Morocco. I was caught up in the moment.

"Nothing, I'm sorry."

"Maybe you should go back to Madrid? I mean, you don't have to stay here with me."

"No, no really, I'll be okay."

Shit, not only was I a lousy lover, I was turning into an unpleasant companion. I felt that sense of panic attacking me, as if I were going to be abandoned, as if I would be asked to pack it in then and there and scoot along. Jesus, what the hell was wrong with me? And what the hell was I doing with this older woman? Maybe she was right, maybe I should go back. But I wanted to stick it out. I was so damn tired of being alone, plus she fascinated me. Lose her? Why didn't I understand about the clitoris? Had my rapturous night in New York City faded away from my memory so completely that I didn't know what to do next? She was using our first night as a hold. I was twenty-four years old and my sex life was a series of intermittent one-night stands or, at best, that week or so with Roberta in San Francisco. I had been captured by Circe and didn't realize it. How was Isabella able to keep a straight face while punishing me with her rites of sex? And how silly I seemed hanging on to her skirts! But her voice was the key to her power. The hero of Joyce's book was trapped by inexperience as well. Like Dedalus, the love of a woman, mother, child and muse was what I so desperately sought in Isabella. I moved in a sea like Ulysses, from estuary to estuary, gaining or losing insights. Isabel, eleven years my senior, had an eighteen-year-old son and a daughter eight years of age from another marriage. Raise the curtain Michael, the proscenium is well lit and the stage is full of creatures, they are glistening from the sticky secretions of the raw unconscious. I was being acquired. Bobbie Hall, a rough-hewn actor spotted Isabel and me one day in Madrid. He summed it up in a flash. "Find someone your own size." It was too late for me; like nicotine, Isabella had entered my veins.

Almost reluctantly we returned to the hotel. She took a bath and I climbed into bed. I wasn't sure if I could or wanted to. She settled it by blithely bouncing to bed and turning the lights off. I thought that that was it, now we could just go to sleep. Isabella was in the mood, but was leaving it up to me to intuit. I dozed off thankful that I did not have to perform. Eventually she grunted a sound that suggested she had wanted it, and why hadn't I? It was too late. She rolled over and went to sleep.

I awoke to pleasant sounds coming beyond our small room, which added to the softness of the moment. I was in a good mood and Isabel looked happy asleep, I would greet the day with my own thoughts. Opening the shutters the deep cerulean sky offered a calm I welcomed. Gazing at the crazy geometry of the small buildings, I felt I had overreacted to Isabel's attempts to move on to wherever we'd go next emotionally. I'd take her shopping. That would be a way to bring things up to the adventure I wanted, a relationship with a beautiful woman. When I woke her I was surprised by the gaiety of her mood; sleep had also refreshed her.

"Come lovely lady, let me take you shopping."

Her smile brought quick tears to my eyes; I turned to avoid her scrutiny.

"Come here, Michael. I want a morning kiss."

An hour later we were bargaining for a golden dress and a cobalt blue robe that I fancied. They were antiques or at least they gave the feel of another time. We had the robes sent back to our hotel. Feeling proud of ourselves we continued to celebrate our affection for each other. Climbing up out of the Medina to the broad boulevards, we felt a kind of triumph. Acquiring these robes created an aura or a grace to our movements. A prince and princess had come alive in the fairytale, which in the streets of the Medina—swept along by the graceful movements of people wearing burnooses—had a biblical texture and a B-movie quality. "Want to buy a diamond?" a tiny man furtively offered as we strolled upwards. This touch of intrigue amused us. The beady-eyed character disappeared before we had a chance to bargain.

"Was that Pepe Le Moco?" Isabel chortled as she wrapped her arm through mine. I shrugged a shoulder and we laughed. We were at least in love with having a good time. In the European quarter, after sending a few postcards, we treated ourselves to a modest lunch sitting at an outdoor café. A well-dressed Moroccan approached our table and asked if he might join us. The man was also in a very good mood; apparently his cousin was getting married that night. It would be a very big wedding and the man surprised us when he insisted we come. "The experience will please you and my cousin would be honoured." Isabel was delighted with the idea. The man said that he would send someone to our hotel to show us the way. The man said it would be better if we were accompanied, that way we would not get lost; it was not far away. We gave him the name of our hotel.

Isabel and I took our dressing up seriously, feeling very much like royal visitors obliged to join in the ceremonial obligations and pleasures of a neighbouring fiefdom. The antique feel of the clothing inspired Isabel to line her eyes with a black accent in the manner typical of women in Morocco. Isabel with kohl-farded eyes looked like a native, sexy and mysterious. The sound of the muezzin promised an exotic evening but the wedding was a static affair. The men and women were separated into two brightly lit rooms. There were no decorations and our host, as well as bride and groom, wore European clothing as did everyone there. Large bottles of whiskey sat waiting on each table and the company sat quietly; it was not the cheerful exuberant festive affair we had anticipated. Several men came by our table and took leering glimpses of Isabel. Neither of us liked being on display and I could feel the whiff of male lust had also upset my princess. Our host came by to offer us whiskey, we thanked him but told him that we had to leave. On our way home we bought some goat cheese, bread and the delicious butter we had discovered and had a quiet picnic in our hotel room.

In Marrakech we found a hotel just off the Jamaa Fna. Our room, accessible from a central courtyard, was completely tiled. It could have made an exotic steam room. She was having a great time. We were treated like royalty everywhere we went! What we had together made us attractive to the outside world! I had never sat in Jamaa Fna at night. Several of the stalls were open. Large mounds of pretzel-like food covered with honey looked rather like a creature from the ocean's depths. They didn't look edible and were less than appealing. We sat down at an open café for some tea. We heard the sound of a horse's hooves and then saw a man wearing jodhpurs and English boots leading his white stallion by the reins. He stopped in front of us. He took a deep bow and then saluted us with the beer that he was drinking. We saluted him and then he offered his horse a swig and saluted us again. We saluted him and he took another swig and saluted again. The stallion turned, a long, glistening pink stamen slid diagonally between his hind legs.

Isabella turned to me. She took hold of my arm, led me down a street, down an alley between the stalls. Isabella lifted her skirt and drew me toward her behind one of the closed stalls. A man walked by, looked at us, and kept going. She was squirming. I was in her. Isabella was on fire. Hot, wet, galloping, we tore at each other. I had never been so hard. Everything went bright, clear, and we were fucking, the machine going full throttle.

"Fuck me, fuck me, fuck me!" The stallion's prick was mine.

"Yes!" Isabella screamed. "Now, now!"

I felt the bolt leaving. It hit and I was still going, like a shuttlecock.

"Oh, good, good, don't stop." Moving in short strokes I began again. Isabella licked the sweat from my eyes, pulling her tongue over the lids. I was hard again. I could feel the sperm in the corridor, cortège of prickly stars. I was now filling the counterfoil, sending telegrams, calling up presidents, signalling to bands, let them begin the parade. Isabella became all beautiful women. She was quiet now, the soft tight gripping of her clingstone, hot fingers stroking like sea anemones, licking the penis, my happy little cock now grown to the dimensions of a colossus.

There was a great silence around us. The sky was popping with glow fish. We stood quiet, together, not moving.

"Isabella, sweet Isabella, look at the stars, they're dancing."

"Puissance, aren't they beautiful?"

"Puissance, puissance, aren't we beautiful?"

Everything was still.

We slipped back into our hotel room and into bed.

"Isabella, let's go to Paris." She lifted an imaginary phone.

"Hello desk, confirm reservations on the next flight."

We, too, were living in the age of teleportation. Milarepa, a Tibetan yogi, and Jesus were the only two to work that one out. H.G. Wells had a time machine and we had kif. Back in Tangiers we bought two kilos then slipped into Spain. That would see us to Paris or wherever.

24

The President's Analyst

In Madrid we went to an American movie, *The President's Analyst*, which was in English with Spanish subtitles, and a real treat. James Coburn was starring and I have always gotten a kick out of his sense of humour. Isabella was up for a good time so we ducked into the darkness to enjoy the nonsense of the film. We started laughing before anyone else in the audience had figured out that this was an absurdist, not a black comedy. The tradition of tongue-in-cheek spy-thriller that helps you digest the popcorn while you escape into the delightful, cocky characterisations of varied government officials too silly to ever be real. Although it sure would be great if they did have just that sense of humour, because reality was even more ridiculous, too ridiculous when they played it for real. Anyway, we made it plain that we knew what was happening, even if the rest of the audience hadn't a clue. How they could have taken this film seriously is beyond belief, but they did. The Spanish audience was taking everything literally and resented our having such a good time with such 'serious' matters. This began to please us just as much as the film. An irate couple behind us even tapped our chairs rather gruffly with an accompaniment of a loud "Shhhh." But we kept on laughing. I was sure that the audience would eventually see that the film was designed as a comedy. Eventually they got it and found something funny and then we were okay, permitted to view the film, permitted to laugh at it.

"Isabella, I think that maybe we are in the wrong country." But what was the right country? America is so beautiful, so rich, the best natural resources, the most beautiful people, so full of hope, so full of innocence... why do we need to have other countries? Why couldn't we have had Buckminster Fuller in the Cabinet with John Lennon? I mean, that's the crazy thing, why couldn't we have a ministry of artists, poets? If we pool our beliefs in the intelligent souls, in the creative beings who have held up those things that have delighted us the most, then what the hell do we need bombs for? I was in the wrong country, but what was the right country? Let's look at it geographically: America is green. It's got natural resources, dramatic, real energy. Let's face it, oh mondo mio, America is the place on the globe that got the best. That's the way it is. So they call it America. Even if there ain't gold in the streets, there is gold in the hearts of the people who live there. But how do we work that out? How can you set up a government that can deal with the world in a very subtle way, in a way that analyses the world's needs? That's what *The President's Analyst* should have been about. That's what I learned at L'École de L'Humanité in Switzerland. "Furthermore, I would like to state" that it would be great to see a country run by artists, not bombs, asshole. I thought about Jim—I saw a grand big powwow. We are not talking Dick Tracy blah-blah, Lenny Bruce, flash my cock, up your ass bullshit. We are talking basic doggie bone, asshole. I hate to lay it out that way, but finally it's just that simple. I was gonna make it Home-free without Mr Bogart. That was my intention. All America needs is love. That was what The Beatles said to America. They came from England after John Kennedy was shot. We don't write history. It happens. Maybe what we need is a contemporary *Spartacus*.

Isabella invited me up to her room for some wine. After a few glasses we fell into laughing and reminiscing about Morocco; it hadn't been that long ago, only two or three weeks. Interestingly, she had seen the trip quite differently than I had. She was much more taken with the 'exotic adventure'. It was a thrilling time, she said. The Moroccan wedding, the hustlers trying to sell us a diamond.

For God's sake, it was a pretty silly film in itself. The man and his horse, bringing back the kif, the cheese on the palm leaf, the belly dancing we had seen just as we were leaving Tangiers, and our buying spree, the robes. My paranoia, yeah, I guess I had taken things too personally. Maybe I had misjudged everything? I asked Isabella if she would like to meet my dad before he left for Rome. She said sure, so I set it up for a coffee late next day.

Who did I think I was kidding? They certainly knew that I was looking for approval, I mean a sort of go-ahead signal. She and I were on time but father was late. I introduced them, they were cordial at first as they tested the waters. I was struck by the fact that neither of them could dominate the other. I think pop's last comment was something to the effect that I was 'his investment'. Isabella immediately sprang to my defence saying I was entitled to my own life. I guess this was just the answer my father was looking for. "Okay, kid, he's all yours," but I didn't get the sense from him that she was the right kind of woman or the wrong kind of woman, and that is what I wanted to hear. I had introduced them to get another sense of our chemistry. What I should have realised was that she was very strong, as dominating as my father, and not such a good 'investment' on my part. As comfortable as it may be to be dominated, it was not really what I needed or wanted. Not seeing this clearly, I reacted to his statement with resentment. I was pushed towards her, so in rebellion I was going to give our relationship the go ahead.

Getting her aroused; I'd found the key to that. The trick was to be alert, so that things went smoothly. We had felt like the King and Queen in Morocco, discounting my uptightness, pseudo-paranoia, and fucking up on a couple of goes in the bedroom. I thought I could handle it now. At least I had had the education. Luckily, that night the spirit of my unconscious took me aside for an intimate *tête à tête*. Jim Morrison, my alter ego, the sexy subconscious cool cat would advise me. In the corner of a dimly lit plush bar he looked regal wearing a neat leather outfit, speaking in the soft tones of poetic irony.

"You know she's a hot number. I mean, to leave her children and split to find herself in Europe and your arms… a cool score."

Jim looked up at the ceiling as if the lines were written between the tiny lights above us, as if he were pulling from the heavens all romantic love. He edged nearer to whisper in my ear.

"It will be a fine ride man. Just be cooooool."

Then he moved away and a mischievous smile illuminated his face. He didn't have to say that my dad was jealous, it was implied.

"I had my eye on you in Morocco. That was a great fuck wasn't it? That is what Norman Mailer was talking about in his essay *The White Negro*."

Jim gave me a slap on the leg.

"You little fuck, you really pulled it off. Dynamite. Hee hee hee."

Jim's figure began floating towards the ceiling, I awoke with an enormous erection.

March drifted into May. Isabella bought a VW bug, I moved in with her, Dad left for Rome; all in all, things seemed to be going well. Isabella and I had a better sexual relationship. We became inseparable. This was great fun because there was so much we wanted to know about each other. We read the same books and discussed them in bed. Her hotel overlooked the Calle Grande and one night we saw a parade of soldiers on horseback. They looked tiny from our window, moving along so neatly like toy soldiers, making us feel very superior. Yeah, I guess we were pretty cool. If for the moment we were drifting in Madrid, we'd find better watering holes elsewhere. Isabella expressed her interest about the north of Spain, Catalonia, Barcelona, the land of Art Nouveau. Dalí and the surrealistic landscape would prove a more enticing environment. Madrid had become bogged down; it closed up early, seemed held to a tepid way of life. We packed up and drove north. Underneath my smug assuredness was a frightened boy. I wasn't good at speaking up. My dad's yelling around the house upset me as a child and as an adult, I felt a nausea. Alone with this woman whose voice was pleasant, it was something to hang on to. I worked at being brave as I had when I was a child and my parents had left to go to Europe. Reality was an emptiness, which I filled with pleasant lies, fabrications and enthusiasm.

25

Living Inside A Gaudí Building – Casa Milà

Barcelona was alive with noise, traffic; we had arrived in the midst of a gala fiesta. The VW was packed to the gills but everyone wanted us to stop, to join in the festivities, to have a drink, to stay. As strangers they wanted us to feel as guests of honour: it was like a big version of Morocco. Two Americans pegged us almost straight off. They wanted us to join them. We were running on nervous energy, but we loved it. A big party, just what the doctor ordered.

The following day we were impatient to explore the city and to find a place to stay. Somehow we nosed our way toward what we would come to know as the centre of town. We were driving up Paseo de Gracia, the main drag, dumbfounded by one building after another. The boulevard was wide and tree-lined, the buildings were packed one against another. It was like going down a row of wedding cakes, each building outdoing the next in a unique expression of Art Nouveau architecture. Shortly after passing a delicate building covered with tiles, we were stopped dead in our tracks by a building that seemed to be undulating. It was built like a fortress, the wall went in and out in a rhythmic pattern, wrought iron danced across deeply recessed windows. The roof had chimneys of tiled towers that resembled Moorish warriors standing guard, their eyes hidden by hoods. She said that that is where she wanted to live. Impossible, I thought, but we decided to check it out.

Inside Casa Milà, a creation of the eccentric Italian architect Antoni Gaudí, we were shown through the pensione by an elderly woman, a hunchback. Her face was pleasant. She showed us two rooms and a bath at the far end of the pensione. These quarters had a private entrance. This was to become the dream castle that I was to touch, feel, and never forget.

"My God, Isabella, look up at that ceiling!" It was a three-dimensional sand dune floating ten feet over our heads. A sharp, serpentine curve ran through it like an eel skimming the top of a lake. Isabella was busy attending to the arrangement of the furniture. I was trying to take it all in. The wainscot went up for about seven feet to shelves and then a faded pink wall climbed to the ceiling.

"Isabella, come here. Look at these doorknobs. They're sculpted."

"Help me with the couch; I don't want to scratch the floor." The floor was parquet designed in a star pattern. Everywhere there were details: the woodtrim around the bevelled doors featured reliefs of shells.

"The bed is good." Isabella was unpacking.

"Come on, Isabella. Take a moment to drink this in."

"Later."

The apartment was like an underwater kingdom, baroque and primordial. The walls were so thick that the sounds from the street were muffled. The trees filtered the light from the outside world, subduing and muting the whole.

"Remind me to get candles," Isabella said as she opened the doors to the bedroom.

"Well, I guess we're in. Let's put up a few lithos and the Joyce figures on the shelves; it will lighten things up some."

"Go ahead. I'm going to explore the pensione. Surprise me," I suggested.

I went down the hallway that joined the rooms. At the end of the hallway was a sitting room. Inside, reading a newspaper was an elegant woman. I introduced myself.

"Hello! Just moving in. Nice to meet you."

"I'm Contessa Montserrat. This pensione has been my home for many years. You like the building?" Her voice was high-pitched.

"It's absolutely overwhelming."

"My uncle commissioned Gaudí to make it. I never thought that I would be living here. Do you know anything about Gaudí?"

"Not a thing."

The sitting room was pleasant, airy.

"He came here and found patrons. There are many buildings in Barcelona that he has built, and there is, of course, the cathedral,

Sagrada Família. Salvador Dalí is now the head of the commission to raise money to complete the structure."

"I see."

"I am here most every afternoon. Come by. We will talk."

"OK."

"You will like it here."

"I'm sure that I will." I shook the Contessa's hand and headed back to our rooms. I liked this lugubrious mansion. It was perfect, and at eighty bucks a month, a bargain. Our living room made a good painting studio.

"Isabella, are you in the bedroom?" She had hung a few lithos and placed the bronzes. My cut-out Joyce figurines looked good against the faded pink. Isabella was resting.

"Join me. Give me a kiss."

As I started to kiss her she grabbed hold of my hair, pushing my head down firmly into the position I would have preferred to come to naturally. She was insistent. I resented this, yet I wanted to please her. She held on to my hair tightly.

"Stay there, please stay."

Eventually I came to feel like a lapdog, and my jaw ached, my tongue lost its energy and my neck gave out. It was as if she sensed that I was at the end of my tether and finally let go and I was able to stop. This was not the Roxanne that my Cyrano was looking for. I felt like a trick in a whorehouse, slipping new images into my mental projector that would help time pass. I was confused with what she wanted and what I expected. To avoid this routine I complied with her escapades at the cafes and restaurants where she could dazzle strangers before returning to the boudoir. Occasionally I'd work in a good fuck, and with my limited education thought that it was something special, which, at the time, it was.

26

Candlelight On Nixon

At the end of our first month in Barcelona, we thought that we'd go up to Andorra, a small principality in the Pyrenees Mountains. It was hot and muggy in Barcelona and we could shop in Andorra, which was duty free. Isabella needed some new blouses and I needed hair oil and other essentials. In Andorra, walking through a covered arcade, we spotted two young American boys. They were just as struck by our appearance as we were by theirs. Sam was tall and husky, his long straight hair making him look like an American Indian; he was boyish, closemouthed and smart but had a glum personality. Ira was short, wore specs and seemed rather frail. You could tell right off the bat that his impression of himself was that he was just as tall as anyone else. Ira was light-footed and talkative, opinionated and 'puckishly' argumentative; in short, just as unlikely a friendship as Isabella's and mine. We got to know each other during the few days of shopping but we left them rather abruptly, giving them our address in Barcelona should they be heading that way.

We were now ready to set up camp and play the game of intellectual American expatriate, existential, exceptional, eccentric. Surrounded by books, lithographs, sculptures, Moroccan rugs, paints, typewriter and notebooks, we viewed the world as our circus. We were the ringmasters. We were the experts who sought out subtle factors that we could exploit to titillate the exotic strings that had been so finely tuned in Morocco at the plazas, in the cafes in Madrid where we had held court, in our thousand-and-one excursions into the world where we had always been hailed as the King and Queen of Bohemia. And who were we playing this for? Ourselves? It was self-indulgent, childish, ...fun. We were seasoned alchemists savouring the most delicious intellectual morsels, picking apart existence, sucking up the marrow of life that whetted an insatiable appetite, that hungered to understand every aspect of human psychology. By the time we had set up in Barcelona we had explored our own limits. We had spent long nights politely tearing at each other, massaging our sexual inability to satisfy each other. Refusing to give any ground, we collapsed on the other end of catharsis, drained of desire. We were tired of fucking each other's brains out; it was time for fresh material.

'Diversion', that was what Ira called it. We had all gone to the Barrio Chino looking for something. We found two young Spanish whores and brought them back to the apartment. We had been drinking Romilar, a cough medicine with codeine. It added a pleasant high, a mild euphoria. Isabella took the two young ladies into the bedroom. She wanted to dress them up, doll them up to make them feel special, to give them a treat. Ira loaded his camera and I put on some music. Moroccan folk songs. Isabella proudly opened the bevelled doors and the three of them came out dancing. Isabella danced with abandon but the two young whores were afraid to tease us; you could feel the control that guarded their having a good time with us. One of the girls permitted Ira to photograph her breasts; giggling she gave him a quick peek. The whole scene felt childish to me. At any rate, it didn't last very long and the whores made excuses and left.

At this point we settled for smoking kif. I usually rolled several joints and Isabel lit the candles, and we gathered around the trunk to weigh the worries of the world, discussing all that we knew and all that we wanted to know. Usually these discussions were dominated by Isabel and Ira; certainly they could out-talk anyone and with kif it was a real onslaught of verbage. Oddly enough, politics, religion and sex outweighed art. Here we were, in the lap of surrealism, discussing Nixon, the war in Vietnam, the stupidity of it all. The romance of Barcelona was held at a distance. Isabel said that she had been gassed in Washington and that that more or less had ended her protesting. Ira always had some nuance to add, a deeper view, he loved the sound of his own voice droning away at a subject. He picked at it delicately from all sides, careful not to exclude some aspect whose implication might alter the whole picture of his argument. He had a need to fill space that drove me up the wall. All Sam and I could do was act as a sort of Greek chorus; permitted a moment to 'yay or nay' a statement, and then Ira would be off again. Moments I wanted to tell the adorable little fart to shut the fuck up. He wasn't the only guy on the planet, for Christ's sake, who had a bellyache.

Ira needed to tell us all about how he had fallen for his English teacher at Buffalo and how they really had a thing going. Then for some reason she had dropped him, just like that. He wanted to probe the reasons, but what could we say? He had been doing some drug dealing and somehow had taken more acid than he had wished to. Did we understand what it was like to be hauled off ignominiously to a police station and shot up with Thorazine against his will? "It was outrageous." How could authority be extended that far, especially since he wasn't hurting anyone? He was experimenting with his own mind—what right did they have to alter it, to snatch him up, against his will and force him to come down, down to their pathetic, mundane, inarticulate, paranoid reality? Ira needed the attention, so we listened. I could see that even Isabella was getting edgy, that Ira's incessant need to hold the stage was beginning to annoy her. And then, he'd give way and she would take over about her life. The difficulty of raising a family with a husband who didn't understand her need for expression; all he wanted was a lay, a dress-up doll he could parade in front of his friends. It was impossible. No matter what she did to try to sensitise him he balked: was this machismo or stupidity? What was an intelligent woman to do? Should she leave her family and find herself? After all, it was her life, not his or her children's.

I was thankful that my own problems—mainly my sex life—were not brought up to this counsel. I'm sure they would have picked apart things I'd just as soon be left alone for me to muse about in the privacy of my own skull. I wasn't used to this sort of public forum. I wasn't sure it really solved anything in any event. It filled time, time I thought could be better spent; my mind looked for projects. What could I do in Barcelona that couldn't be done elsewhere?

27

A Dalí Dream, Soft Time

In the mornings Isabella wanted the apartment to herself to do some writing. After I'd gone downstairs for a bottle of coffee and milk, she was free to rake over her notebooks for several hours while I went out to shop for food in the large covered market downtown. It was a fascinating expansive market filled with fresh fish, fruit and cheese and hundreds of other items particular to Spain. Often it was a guessing game to figure out what these items might be used for. Ira took photos: a beautiful bouquet of sardines laid out in a fanning shape over a woven plate, people standing on the corner, the newspaper man who sat in an odd contraption that he presumably folded up tight at the end of the day made for unusual subjects.

Ira away from Isabella was more tolerable. The need to dominate the soirée having passed, he became a more low-key fellow whose touches of humour or irony were profound. This however was only when he wasn't bellyaching about something being 'outrageous'. I liked Ira. I genuinely found his whole 'act' rather diverting myself.

It was midsummer. What was the harm if we were having a good time speculating about projects, taking little trips, imbuing ourselves with life in Barcelona, sitting outside on the spacious walkways sipping our drinks thinking about Gaudí? Wouldn't it be mind-blowing to do a really big, deluxe, full-colour coffee table photo book on all of his wonderful architecture? None of us had as yet seen one; we'd looked in several bookstores. Our conversation would hold for a while and then as the day began to close and we went to El Drugstore Restaurant, we'd be on to other subjects. Our zany ideas kept coming. The characters on The Ramblas—a low-life study, the Spanish version of Forty-Second Street New York City. We imagined shades of Genet and John Rechy's *City of Night*. The comings and goings of hippies and rucksack wandering wonderers were other tempting possibilities. It was the bohemian travellers, and the long-termers like the poet with two thumbs, that especially spoke to us. Ira and I would do the photos and drawings. Isabella could do the text. It was speculation to fill time. Something would come to mind that was even better, more enticing.

Certainly, Gaudí got the most votes. We all loved Park Güell. An 'Alice in Wonderland' estate, now a public park built with numerous personal touches we delighted in. Aside from the tiles that covered the gatehouses and the long, curvilinear cement bench that skirted the large plaza where young children played soccer, there were the odd touches, like the huge carved balls that Gaudí had placed under the palm trees which changed shape with the passing light of day. There was also an ominous tunnel, an arcade underneath the plaza shaped like a teardrop placed on its side. The inside tunnel of a large wave, a hallway to infinity. Park Güell would have made a fine subject for a book we might have worked on. The park was not closed up at night. Sometimes we would take a drive to get away from the smoke-filled living room where we spent our nights poring over ideas as the wax of the candles gradually spread its arms over the coffee table, surrealistically welcoming the dawn, a moment heralded by the clopping of the horse-drawn milk cart sluggishly passing below toward the morning light.

By way of the grapevine (actually through Ira's contact with other artists) we learned about an opening that Dalí was giving in support of Gaudí's cathedral, which was still unfinished. Dalí was on the committee to help raise the funding that would eventually complete the building. I thought this was in character, Mr Dalí being a surrealist and interested in crucifixion. The architecture: bodies melting into columns, ecstatic revelations and the like. All of us got so excited by the prospect of actually meeting Dalí, that we fumbled the time and missed the event. I felt responsible, so I suggested that we hop in the car and drive up to see him; it would be better that way, a private audience, so to speak. It was pretty well known that he lived near Cadaqués, which was just up the coast, some fifty miles north of Barcelona.

There was still plenty of daylight when we arrived at his estate, which sat facing a lake that looked as if it had been raised up several feet creating the impression that is so familiar in Dalí's landscapes. His otherworldly visions were right outside his front door. None of us would have suspected such a fact. We rang his doorbell but there was no answer. The walled-in estate was quite fantastic. The front façade was French in feeling and behind its high fence we could see a dome that looked like a large egg. There were several large trees in front and a small unassuming boat moored to a tiny dock. The lake seemed to be jacked up, as I've said, the horizon tilted up; the perspective was strange, the silence unnerving. Nature was a good watchdog.

We rang the doorbell again and waited. The silence was soon broken by the sound of footsteps.

"Momento, por favor."

"Signor Dalí"

"El no estará aqui, venido más esta noche. Venga, hasta, hasta, OK?"

And so we had been invited to a party. What a thrill but there were several hours before nightfall. We would have to amuse ourselves, which wouldn't be too difficult observing our surrealistic surroundings. Satisfied with the immediate environs we decided to head out and explore the terrain. It was a curious landscape. As we drove about the land tilted one-way and then another. It was a monotonous ride and we thought it was time to return, even if we had to wait for dark before presenting ourselves at Dalí's door. Actually I don't know what I expected to say to him, his world being so far removed from my own, at least in terms of the work that I was doing. Had we been going to see Fellini I'd have been more comfortable; I adore his work, it was my Roman childhood, my backyard. Dalí's limped world of sagging flesh and distant horizons, exaggerated compositions, windows in bodies, created a bloated decadent world, diseased and fascinating like the burning giraffes running in waves I once saw in a private collection. Dalí was the figure who had appeared one day when I was sitting on a beach under the influence of LSD. He had lifted up the ocean at the shore as easily as a sheet of paper. It would be unlikely that I'd have the presence of mind or his attention to relate these experiences to him. I never liked to go greet someone empty-handed or empty-minded.

It got dark quickly and the moon lit the terrain giving it the appearance of a lunar surface. It was so mesmerizing that we got lost and spent the night trying to find the right road back to Dalí's castle. Morning found us in Cadaqués ravenously eating fresh bread, straight from an old clay oven. We had smelled the bread baking and followed the scent up a small path. We ate the bread as the sun began to warm the steps where we were sitting. We had driven through a Dalí dream, soft time.

28

Cauliflower Opera

Sam returned to the States, which left just the three of us. For a while Ira left the fold and Isabella and I were able to spend time alone. We had been so busy running around that it was now pleasant just to be with each other. For the moment we were content. Isabella worked quietly in the alcove writing while the soft light that filtered through the colourful paisley cloth over the window created a peaceful atmosphere. I began painting in the living room. Occasionally, she would ask me to listen to some of her notes. They were poetic but somewhat fragmented. They hinted at a larger work where I hoped she would draw more conclusions about her feelings. They didn't reflect the sense of excitement that she was so good at stirring up, a Roman candle so short fused and quick. The delicate observations that she was recording were lovely, but they weren't Isabella. Perhaps her letters to her friends took care of those flights of energy; she never shared her letters with me, so I really don't know.

Our sex life had mellowed. Neither of us complained. Our excursions reflected a new understanding. One morning we went to visit the newly opened Picasso Museum. It was located in the oldest section of town and we had an inspiring time looking at his graphic works, which made me hungry to do more prints. I had gotten my feet wet in Madrid. Leaving the museum we sauntered down the street speaking of Picasso. We drifted into an old church. Isabella and I had this cavernous space to ourselves. The floor was empty but a large shaft of light struck the top surface of a plain stone altar. The altar had surely been placed there for the very effect it was now creating. On the altar, glowing in the light was a gold wedding band.

I took the ring and placed it on Isabella's finger.

"Marry me!"

"Michael, don't be silly."

I grabbed Isabella and kissed her, pressing her close. "Marry me, Isabella!" I was lifting her skirt; maybe that would do it.

She stopped me.

"Michael, we barely hold it together now, how would it be if we got married?"

"You're running away, always leaving."

"That's not it at all. You want too much, Michael."

"If we settled down everything would be fine."

Isabella playfully suggested a solution. "OK. Let's pretend we just got married."

"Pretend doesn't do it. Aren't you the one who always says that almost doesn't count?" I took her head in my hands and kissed her gently. "Please, Isabella. All this is driving me crazy."

"It won't work. We're both too unsettled. Maybe when we are old we can get together and tell our stories." She kissed me sweetly.

"I don't want to wait that long."

"Michael, that is the best time." She turned and started to walk away.

"Isabella, wait. OK, let's pretend. Let's see if it makes any difference."

What freedom was Isabella holding on to? Didn't everyone, upon seeing us out together, assume that we were married, anyway? Weren't we treated like royalty of Bohemia? I mean, there was a special chemistry that existed between us that made people stand up and take notice. There was nothing wrong with that. That wasn't why I wanted her to commit. I wanted to settle something in her, that restless energy, that almost tortured search for something that seemed to come between her and my sense of ease. That was the instigator that drove us apart. The restless, unfulfilled demons that drove her out into the world for adventures. And if I was always the best, the most interesting, then why wouldn't she just give in so that we could really go ahead and have real goals instead of these plans that never seemed to get off the ground. There was nothing wrong with these projects; they were great if only we could attack one of them. I blamed that demon inside of her. The petulant spoiled brat that wanted more, wanted new, wanted and wanted and wanted. Ira was waiting for us back at the apartment. He had found his own genius, an artist that he wanted us to meet.

Bill Collins resembled Tony Perkins in *Psycho*; long shoulders and effeminate attempts at composure. His studio, a crowded apartment, was packed with an assortment of varied works. Truncated banisters in white painted boxes, small collages and dolls with strands of glass tubing and springs coming gaily out of the tops of their heads. Bruce Conner in San Francisco had used dolls more effectively, placing them under dense webbing in baby carriages. Collins' work was decorative by comparison. It certainly wasn't something I needed to explore just then.

Bill gushed over Isabella. In a funny and indirect way Ira was making his own comment about us by introducing us to Bill.

"You must let me take you to the opera."

"Oh?"

Collins offered us white wine. I kept looking at the toy dolls with strands of string and glass tubing coming out of their heads, strange bouquets of innocence destroyed, an obvious metaphor, I thought.

"The season starts tomorrow. I usually go with a Contessa, my patron. She would be so surprised to see me with someone else."

I was not enthusiastic about this guy courting Isabella right in front of me, but I knew that if I showed jealousy, she would be annoyed. I didn't think him dangerous; it was his wounded bird attitude that pecked at me, and his summation of humanity.

"Why don't you come over tomorrow for tea? We'll see how things go," chirped Isabella.

I had just proposed to her this morning. This was a slap in my face.

"That will be lovely. I'll have a chance to see Michael's work. Ira has told me so much about it." Collins emitted an insipid mannerism, the kind of flattery that I loathed.

"I wait all year for the opera season to start. It is my one chance to make a social appearance. Otherwise, I go to Germany to sell works. Here I am patient."

He kept pushing the notion that an artist must never push a sale, must appear secure, ask for nothing.

"You aren't the only one, Charlie," I was thinking. Now I had another idiot to deal with. It wouldn't have been so bad if Collins had had an original thought to his credit. All this was another waste of time. He was quite excited about the possibility of Isabella going with him to the opera. I could just see him introducing her to the other empty-headed people that he courted for sales. Ask for nothing.

Shit! He was using my Isabella for his bait. I was steaming.

"See you tomorrow, about four o'clock."

"Fine. Ciao."

"Bye-bye."

We drove back and Ira expected to be invited up to continue discussing his discovery. "Not tonight, Ira. Isabella and I want to be alone." She seemed surprised by my directness. I wanted to remove all distractions, to turn my own hourglass. I turned on the tub for a bath. Isabella came in and joined me.

"I need a vacation from this vacation," I said. "Come here. Give me a kiss. I've been a good boy today."

"I can't argue with that." She came close and we kissed tenderly. We started to stroke one another.

"Come on. Out of the water."

"We just got in."

"So what?"

"Aren't you being the tough guy?"

"It's about time, baby." I playfully threw her on the bed and started her pleasure. I wasn't going to do it all night, either. After the first swoon I mounted her and we started rolling.

"Oh, Michael, that feels so good. Faster, love, faster."

"Shut the fuck up for a change."

"Oh yes, yes! That's it! Fuck me hard."

"You quixotic fucking cunt. I love you. I love you, Isabella."

"Michael! Yes, yes, I'm coming! Come, baby, come."

I did. And bounced out of bed.

"That was the best, Michael, really the best."

"I'm hungry," I realised out loud.

"There are some things inside, love. Do you want me to go and look?"

"No, my dear, it will be my pleasure!"

Inside the living room I grabbed a few things and headed back to the bedroom. Isabella was beaming. She was the happiest that I had ever seen her. We began eating and I opened a jar of marinated cauliflower. I was hot, and went to the window to cool off. I felt triumphant. At the window the night air covered my naked body. The cauliflower didn't taste good, so I threw it out the window as if I were tossing flowers at a parade. Isabella was laughing.

The following afternoon Collins appeared on schedule, all dolled up—no pun intended—in a pressed suit and with a flower in his lapel. We sat down for tea and kif. Collins resisted at first, but Ira talked him into it. After a few hits he got up to comment on my work, posing as a big art critic. He had a degree from Harvard. He was implying that my work was derivative. Isabella pointed out that the lithographs were intended as a spoof. They were supposed to be reminiscent of Renoir, Vuillard and Lautrec; they were an impressionist view of Joyce. Collins was not enjoying the Pop Art fun of it. I could see that Isabella was giving him a lot of rope.

"Bill, what do you think of Louise Nevelson?" Bill's reliefs were literally straight out of a Nevelson textbook.

"She's OK," Collins replied, curtly dismissing Isabella's question.

"Strange. I would have thought that you would adore her; there's such a strong empathy between your work and hers."

"Do you really think so?" Ira and I could smell the kill coming.

"Funny. I guess you have a lot in common with Braque."

"I don't understand?"

"If you were to put Braque and Picasso side by side, the Cubist period, the early works, you couldn't tell them apart."

"Are you suggesting that my works are similar to Nevelson's?" Collins was getting the drift.

"No, Bill. I'm saying that your work is a direct copy of it."

Collins threw back his head and made a beeline for the door. We watched him from the window.

"Give our regards to the Contessa, Mr Nevelson." Collins ignored Isabella's comment. He threw out his arm, looking at his watch. He was in a hurry to get to the opera. Ira had lost a friend but I felt championed!

"To hell with Collins. I've worked up an appetite. Can't get a meal off his beaver butt ass." I didn't much want to gloat over the charade; I was tired of it.

"C'mon, let's go to our favourite restaurant."

"Opera, Mike?" Ira realised Collins' pretentiousness.

"You betcha, Ira."

"Opera, opera... the problem with Barcelona, man, is that there aren't any rock concerts."

"Yeah, tell me about it." Ira and I headed down the stairs under Gaudí's faded romantic murals.

"You know, it would be great to go to a Doors concert. Buffalo was a mindblower... gave away a lot of acid... what a blast."

"Barcelona ain't Buffalo, buddy," I said, feigning Bing Crosby. "So how was the concert?"

"Outrageous. Morrison is a terrific shaman."

"I like Jim," I said. "We spent time together. We were pretty close before he got into singing."

"No shit!"

"Sweet LA, surrealistic LA. My mom fed us one day." I leaned over, letting Isabella in. "Just telling Ira about my days with Morrison."

"Who?" she asked.

"A school buddy who became a rock'n'roller."

"Carry on. Want me to sit in the back?" Ira asked.

"No, that's OK." Isabel interjected.

"So, Mike, what was he like in those days?"

"Quiet... I don't know. There was a sense of something hidden behind those mysterious eyes of his..."

"Like what?"

"I don't know really... a quality of wonderment! I think that's what made him so appealing; his thoughts were unique. He was a poet, always pointing out things in a vaguely precise way."

"Yeah... so what did you guys do together?" Ira wanted some dirt.

"We went for rides, trips. Jim pointed out beauty and helicopters."

"Fuck, man, what else is there?"

"You've got a point there, Ira."

We had arrived at our destination, a working-class place. The food was delicious. "I don't see the boys around." Isabella was referring to Ira's other friend, the painter who adored Dalí and his sidekick who adored heroin. "Yeah, I haven't seen them lately. I think Todd went to Paris." Ira was depressed.

"C'mon, Ira, cheer up! Collins is an asshole," Isabella interjected.

"I wasn't thinking about Collins. I was thinking about the winter." Ira paused for a moment. "I think England needs me. I'm so damned tired of all of this foreign yapping. I need to talk to people who understand me."

"Chicken or fish?" I asked, hoping that we could move on towards getting some food into our bellies.

"Fish and chips, mate." Ira's mood had lifted.

"What did we have the last time that we were here?" Isabella asked. She was hungry, too.

"Pastrami," Ira announced.

"Yeah… wouldn't that be nice?" Ira could be very cute.

"I should have asked Hamilton to bring us some."

"Who?" Ira and I were both thrown.

"Oh, sorry. With all the excitement I forgot to mention that Bill Hamilton is coming for a visit."

"Isabella, are you kidding, or what?" I had heard her mention Hamilton before. He had been her last boss, a filmmaker. They had been on a shoot and he had chosen to save his camera rather than her. A train had unexpectedly appeared and he had grabbed his camera, leaving Isabella to her own devices. Of course, nothing tragic had occurred, but she had interpreted the situation, making Hamilton the heavy.

"When?"

"I think tomorrow afternoon. I didn't invite him. He insisted on a visit."

"I thought you'd had enough of him."

"I have. He won't take no for an answer and has to check it out firsthand for himself."

"Check *what* out?"

"Don't get uptight, Michael. It's just a friendly visit."

"Four thousand miles out of his way just for a hello… not what I would call a friendly visit."

"Look: if you're going to be that way it's fine, that's on you. As far as I'm concerned, the same goes for him. Move out for a few days. It would make things easier."

"What things?"

"We don't need a three-ring circus, do we?"

I said nothing.

"I don't want him to know that we're living together. It will only complicate things. Maybe we can try to sell him some of your work."

"Thanks." So I was going to meet Isabella's private correspondent. I couldn't believe it; all that she'd ever indicated to me had been that the guy was a schmuck. When would this horseshit end?

"Look, Michael, don't make a big deal out of this. Bill doesn't mean anything to me. Don't give me that jealous look; it's hateful. Don't do it to me and don't do it to yourself. I have an obligation to a relationship I once had with a man."

"You want to end it gracefully and give it all the poison that it deserves."

"He's not going to be staying with me. He's going to be rooming down the hall."

I got up. "Where are you going, Michael?" Isabella asked me as I turned to leave. Ira joined me outside. "Hey, man, why don't you move in with me for a few days? We'll have fun watching Isabella clip this chump's wings."

"I'm not in the mood."

"C'mon, Mike. Don't play the wounded lover." He slapped me on the back as we went for the car.

Driving back to the apartment, I wasn't listening to Isabella or Ira. I was sorting things out. Where was my life? I needed to get back to work. What was it that kept me pinned to Isabella? I adored her, but she was consuming me. She had a dominating personality and a talent for making it seem that it was my choice to stick it. "Come on, Michael. Don't look so glum. Ira will help you pack your toothbrush."

"Thanks, ma. I'd rather do it myself."

Naturally I felt hurt, not betrayed—that was too strong—but deeply hurt. But I had promised myself to give in to whatever Isabella wanted, no matter... just to see if in the end she wouldn't give in to my request to be my wife. I think that if I'd had any sense at all I would have just thrown in the towel then and there, but by then her hooks were in too deeply. Besides, this new development would soon clear up everything one way or the other once and for all.

"Stop that crap, Michael. You'll like Bill. He's upbeat."

"We'll see, won't we?"

I walked Ira to his pensione, which was right around the corner.

"Listen, Ira," I said, "I've had enough dialogue for one night."

"Don't get sore at me. I'm not responsible for your sex life."

"Some sex life, huh?"

"Why don't you split, man? Come to London with me. Isabella's impossible. You are never going to contain all of that energy. It's great fun for me, but I'm not living with her. You need another kind of woman. I know, man, I know. You don't want to hear this. But look at what's going on. You haven't done any work in months. You're hooked on her and it's dragging you down."

The room I got for the night was a closet. The window was as big as the door and I was afraid to make a mistake and plummet from my bedroom.

"Want to smoke some kif with me?" Ira had his pipe loaded and ready to be lit. It had come from our stash, mine and Isabella's; we had enough that we could afford to be generous with it.

"No, I think I'll turn in. Like they say, tomorrow is another day."

"Give a thought to London, would you?"

"Right."

What the hell was I doing in this tiny room, in this tiny world? I had close to nine hundred bucks left over from the five thousand I had earned for the sculptures that I had done for Phil Yordan's Peruvian saga. I could make that nine hundred last just as easily in London. I repeated the thought to myself in an attempt to convince myself, but deep down I knew that until Hamilton had made his move, nothing would get me on a plane away from her. I spent most of that evening imagining the poacher Hamilton: his dress, his appearance and his plans to dethrone me.

29

The Three Ring Circus

The Hamilton that I met the following afternoon was the professional type that I always find intimidating: tall, waspish, the kind of cordial chap that gets everything out of life that he wants. What I seemed to forget is that this type of all-American usually lacks humour. For him everything is serious and on schedule; no whiff of Jewish fatalism that seems to give us an edge in the soul department. He is the boy next door, the redhead, the dreamboat in the eyes of all the shiksas.

That's OK too, like my friend Forrest, he would give me the shirt off his back, would go to bat for me under impossible circumstances, never suggesting that I am asking too much of his friendship, because he knows that I would do the same for him. You might say that he was competitive that way. Somehow I knew that I wouldn't be extending this credit to Hamilton.

"I like your work, Michael. Isabella had been telling me how impressed she is. I am too, I must say. You've done a lot for a young man."

"Thanks, Bill. Isabella tells me that you make documentaries." I was trying to keep it short and sweet.

"Well, let's talk about you. What are your plans?" Hamilton looked pompous. I'd observe the situation. I stepped back from being the bust out enfant terrible. Ira was blunter about his feelings. As far as he was concerned, the guy was a schmuck, travelling four thousand miles to visit a madhouse.

What struck me as funny was that Hamilton and Isabella were viewing me as their progeny rather than as a potential suitor. I went along for the ride. She became surprisingly flippant toward me. She had acquired my works, so to speak. I guess Hamilton thought nothing of a friendly shtup thrown in; that was more or less the way the artist was expected to say thank you. That was what I imagined Hamilton was thinking, because I could tell almost immediately that he had no concept about artists whatsoever. Was Barcelona stimulating? And how did I see myself in the relationship with the local movements, if at all? Isabella was beaming now; I was her protégé. I hated the spot. Hamilton could care less. He was here for only one thing, of that I was sure.

"I'm trying to get back to work. There are a lot of distractions in Barcelona," I said bluntly.

"It's a great city. Isabella was telling me about Park Güell. Isn't that right, dear?"

Dear. Just great. Isabella was taking it all in. Maybe Hamilton was the real McCoy and I was just the summer diversion to fill time while they sorted things out. Just then I didn't care to finalize my thoughts. Who knows? Maybe they would ride into the sunset together. Hamilton could look after her much better than I, indulge her creativity, encourage her writing. I was good at that, but only up to a point. Isabella was a brilliant conversationalist, he could tutor her and with the added ambiance of the university to which he was connected, they could have a neat academic sense of being in the arts. The life of an artist is uncertain; freedom is a difficult job.

"I'm sure that you didn't come here to see Park Güell."

"That's right, Michael. I came here to ask Isabella to marry me."

"Isn't that a bit premature, Bill?" Isabella inquired.

"Darling, I've decided. And you know, Bill Hamilton…"

I had to laugh. There was a knock at the door.

"I'll get it." Isabella opened the door and admitted Ira.

"I don't see what's so funny, Michael."

"Stick around, Bill. The circus is in town. Isabella, where is the whip?"

"That's a cocky remark, Michael," Hamilton offered in a deepened tone of voice.

I could see that this guy had no sense of humour. Isabella wasn't going to change. Whoever wound up with her would have to deal with her shenanigans.

There would always be someone coming over to visit. Fuck it. I was going to have some fun. I deepened my voice: "Mr Hamilton, we have considered your qualifications and…"

"You little snot." Bill was upset.

"C'mon, Bill, dear. Michael doesn't mean anything by that. It's just…"

"Isabella, I'll handle this," Bill intoned.

"Listen, Bill, why don't you save all the hot air for the *Kraft Theater*. We don't watch TV over here." I felt good. Why should I put up with this asshole. I didn't give a shit about Isabella's precious feelings, either.

"Michael, what's come over you?" she asked.

"Me?"

"Young man, you'd better leave now."

"After you, Charlie."

"Listen, kid…"

"Don't call me kid, asshole."

With that Bill came forward. He raised his hand as if to slap me and I caught it in mid-air. It stunned him. "You little shit," he growled.

"Hey, Mike, c'mon, man. Leave the old folks alone," Ira interjected.

"Shut the fuck up, man," I said.

"Michael, stop this. This is no way to behave," Isabella shouted.

Bill had fire in his eyes. I let go of his hand. Isabella came forward and pushed me aside.

"Michael, I want you to leave this instant."

I looked at her. She looked serious and ridiculous.

"Come on, man," Ira almost pleaded.

I turned and headed out the door. Ira followed.

"Fucking lunatic asylum!" I was smiling. I had been doing a bit of acting of my own.

"Forget it, man." Ira was trying hard to distract me with a large dose of enthusiasm.

"Hey, listen. Let's do a Doors concert here in Barcelona. You know, hell, take advantage of the friends that you have. What do you say? Fuck, Morrison would really blow them away here. God, it would be great. The Doors in Barcelona. We would travel with them. I could document the concerts. We would tour Europe in style. If you like, I'll get a letter up to them and check out an arena?"

"Ira, shut the fuck up!"

"Sorry, man. Why didn't you say something?"

"Where are we going, anyway, Ira?"

"Come on, Mike. Let's smoke some kif and plan the Morrison tour, how 'bout that? Come on, Bucko!" Ira was beaming with hope. He looked so funny that I had to laugh.

"OK, you. Let's show this town a good time."

We headed up to Ira's to plan the attack.

The following day, fate decided to play her cards. Towards evening, Isabella became ill. She had terrible pains in her side. I had stopped by to say hello and to see how things were going. Where in the hell was Hamilton? In his room, I was informed, which was right down the hall. I didn't understand why he hadn't called a doctor. He was angry with Isabella and besides, he didn't speak Spanish. For Christ's sake doctor is the same word in Spanish—the guy is a schmuck. I had to do something. Feeling her head I could tell she had a high fever. I hustled down the hall and asked our Contessa for the name of a few good doctors. I called two of them. The first one tried to give her a shot. He couldn't manage it somehow. While I was considering taking Isabel to a hospital, the second doctor showed up. He was a surgeon and spoke good English. He was young and his manner reassuring. He had no trouble telling that she had acute appendicitis and gave her a shot. He said that he would operate the following morning and I should bring her to the hospital. The operation went well. Late in the afternoon I visited Isabella who was still groggy. She felt good and said I should keep Hamilton away for a day or so. I calmed her, I told her don't worry, just relax, and concentrate on getting better.

30

Powwow With Jim

I went to fill Bill in. Isabella thought it would be a good idea if we got to know each other better. Bill agreed. I returned to the pensione where I was now staying and conferred with Ira. I felt tired, I went to my room, the box. Enough space to fit a bed and a chest of drawers. I was sleeping in a vault, a coffin. Dozing off, I thought perhaps I should really try to patch things up between Hamilton and Isabella, and bow out.

"Not on your life, man. This is when the game gets interesting."

Of course my sexual mentor had to put in his two cents. There was Jim. Morrison stood on the window ledge and glared at me.

He jumped down, took a step and sat at the end of my bed.

"This is when you got to pull back, just watch what is happening. This is the fun part. Get your ego out of it and your cock as well. This is the time to stick a licked finger in the air to feel which way the wind is blowing. The hell with Hamilton and Isabel, you have to feel your own power, feel your own animal attraction at work or you is dead fish baby, and you ain't no son to Marc Lawrence either."

"What do you mean by that crack?"

"You're so dumb sometimes Lawrence, I don't know why I bother."

When Jim called me Lawrence I knew he meant what he said. There were tears in my eyes but my heart grew strong.

"I'll be Ulysses and sweep the suitor away," I said out loud but there was no one to hear me. A rattle of wind banged the window, my advisor had left the arena.

The following morning I was surprised to see Hamilton walking out of the hospital as I was arriving. Isabella was drying tears away from her eyes and she cried again because she was relieved to see me.

"Michael, Michael, I love you so much, I really do, please don't leave me."

Drying her face with the Kleenex she added, "He's so stupid, so cruel."

"What did he say?"

"It doesn't matter, it's you I love, my Michael from Morocco. Come here, hold me," Isabel pleaded.

Next to her I could smell the pleasant odour of antiseptics, and I asked if it was alright to sit down. It wouldn't hurt her if the bed moved.

"No, Michael, I love you so much."

Sitting there looking into her eyes, stroking her on the head, she asked me to stand up. I got up and stood by her. She unzipped my fly.

"What are you doing?"

"Shhh… just let me."

She put my penis in her mouth. I felt the warm presence of her tongue. It felt good and I relaxed. Soon there was a knock at the door.

"Just a moment," I said.

It was too late to stop. I came and quickly zipped up just as the doctor came in. The timing was such that the doctor probably intuited what had happened. He said nothing about it, only that Isabella could go home tomorrow and that she should take it easy. In a week or so she would be more or less back to normal. He wished us well and left. Isabella was calm and I sat with her for a while and then told her that I'd pick her up early. I'd go back now to clean up the apartment. I kissed her goodbye. At the door, I turned and saw her looking out the window. Leaving the hospital, I realised that was the first time that Isabella had gone down on me.

I hadn't thought I'd win the battle. I had suspected that she'd return to Bill Hamilton. Just then I felt rather dumb just like Jim had said, as I mused about the good times: how we loved to laugh as we applauded the Guardia passing in the park. How he had kept his dignity, ignoring our jesting by his rigid striding. Hadn't we been amused at the polished soldiers galloping by on horseback all in a row and how they looked like little metal toy soldiers because we were five stories up and high on kif. Wasn't life all a parade, a ridiculous parade held to conventions that we could see through? Why could we see everything so clearly and fail to understand our own small circus? And good sex, that feeling of passivity, of opening, of letting things go, the whoosh, the flow, the stream of rich hot life passing along the corridors, dancing and singing, acrobats and madmen, clowns and adventurers, sportsmen and poets, tumbling over one another, laughing and crying, leaving forever their small round sanctuary, that was the feeling we wanted to clothe ourselves in and give back to the world through our art. Maybe, after Hamilton left we'd finally straighten things out. Maybe all the anguish was behind us and we'd be able to inspire one another, wasn't that what we really wanted to do?

Back at Casa Milà I was surprised by Bill's presence in the apartment. He was finishing up his morning exercises. He explained that he hadn't room to do them in his tiny quarters. He said that he had gotten a form of mouth cancer and he was obliged to exercise each day. It was okay now, if he just kept to his regimen. I said that Isabella was coming home tomorrow morning and that if he wanted to use the flat he had better do so early. Fine, fine, that was okay, he said, mopping himself dry. I said I was going to clean up the apartment and he said he was just going. My sense of what was normal, and what was normal for Bill Hamilton was different than my experience with Isabel. I thought I saw things clearly, but when you are so close, clarity is too subjective. I could have cut Bill some slack, explored his feelings and motives, but I was too self involved, selfish. So reality would probably take another spin.

31

The Mirror Without A Face

I brought Isabella home. She wanted to be alone, which felt okay. I could understand her wanting to readjust to the apartment. I simply excused myself and walked down Calle Grande. It was time to settle myself, breathe in the air and empty out the mind. It had been a long time since I'd taken a real moment for myself, months. I had had enough stimulation to last me, who knows, maybe a lifetime. For a moment, an odd thought stuck me. What if I were to just keep walking? I was enjoying my own company. I had transposed my feelings for my father to Isabella. She too offered a blanket of security. What a strange notion. I remembered that Isabella had suggested that in some way we married one of our parents. Isabel was home now resting. I was spending the day quietly, building my strength.

Returning to Isabella's apartment, I found Hamilton with an open bottle of Fundador cognac in his hand. He was shitfaced. He greeted me as if I were an old friend. I knew things had gone too smoothly. Hamilton hung on me and insisted that I take a drink. Isabella looked at all of this but said nothing. Bill took a swig and then shoved the bottle into my hand. Shit it was a bad Hemingway movie! Hamilton was blathering away about how sorry he is, sorry that he had been such a fool, sorry that he had made a pain in the ass out of himself. Hamilton collapsed entirely, bawling like a baby. I was holding him trying to console him as best I could, telling him I was sorry too. It was a lie, but I was frightened. I was waiting to see if his mood would turn around, maybe Bill would explode, but this didn't happen. Hamilton had been broken.

Isabella spoke up.

"Help him to his room."

I tried to get him up. I realised that he was at the point of passing out. I couldn't manage it alone. Isabella had to help me get him on his feet. We managed to get him back to his room. Isabella opened his door and then split—abruptly, I felt. Making my own way back to the apartment the floor was tilting, Jesus, that stuff was strong. Using the wall as a crutch I managed the fifty feet back into the apartment where Isabella was standing waiting for me. She helped me to the bedroom and said that she'd be right back. My head was reeling, the room kept circling. Not feeling any nausea, the experience entertained me. Isabella came back with a doctor. She had him give Hamilton a shot to knock him out and to avoid severe alcohol reaction. She wanted to know how I felt. I thought I was okay. The doctor left. Hamilton would stay out and she doubted whether we'd even see him again. And that was exactly the way it went—no goodbyes.

The following morning after his departure, I thought things were settled and Isabella and I could get down to something. Art for a change of pace. She had some feather up her ass about the way I had handled Hamilton. She said we acted like two lovers. This really pissed me off. For Christ's sake, the guy was drunk, what was I supposed to do, slug him? What did it matter at that point? Finally I got it: Isabella hadn't had a chance to twist the knife in. Wouldn't she let anything go? Did she have to emasculate the whole world? She had just escaped with her life, and she was back at it. One moment of giving, the moment that she put my penis in her mouth, that was it. My brilliant companion was a childish brat who had to have the last word.

I took the VW and headed out toward the country. I just kept driving.

Toward mid-afternoon, I stopped for a rest. By this time I was in the country.

Was I really going to leave her or was I just running away from home? I opened Breton's book on Surrealism—as if I hadn't had enough of the real stuff. I let Breton absorb the tension. A photo in the Breton book I was gazing at brought to mind an evening in LA. I

had rushed to attend the opening of Ed Kienholz's sculptural environment of Barney's Beanery bar, installed right next to the actual bar. I wanted to meet the artist and I did; he was sitting in a nonchalant fashion wondering why I was dashing about so. His quizzical expression was inviting. Maybe I'd amused him. Jim Morrison met me at the door. He had been at the actual bar and had come out to get some air to find me standing there. We went into Kienholz's replica of the bar which presented people sitting at a dimly lit bar in a tight tube. The mannequin figures sat at the bar with drinks and cigarettes, their heads had been replaced with clocks wearing hairpieces. Polyester resin had been poured freely over their shirts and wigs: it was the dialogue that wasn't spoken, a syrupy glue that bound humanity in its surreal connections. Barney himself dressed in his Hawaiian shirt had the only actual head and behind him was the sign, 'Fags stay out', which was also in the actual bar, though no-one paid much attention to it.

Jim commented, "This is all cool except for the sign. Sometimes they can be annoying. Sometimes they need to hang on me, like you hang on Isabella."

"I don't see it that way," I said in my daydream.

"Look pal, it's your game. Frankly, I don't see what you see in her. She's sucking everything out of you. What are you doing? I mean, are you doing any painting? No, you are managing her time. You could do that for me and get paid for it." The smell of the polyester resin overwhelmed me. I led us outside. Funny... he wanted to look after me, he wanted me around. Even the Jim of my daydream made sense. Maybe it was a premonition, maybe he was actually in Europe. The hair at the back of my neck felt the chill of reality. I closed the book and drove back.

It would have been preferable if we had had the kind of experiences that Red Grooms and Mimi seemed to have had travelling to Yugoslavia, visiting the Byzantine mosaics, or doing puppet shows travelling in Italy. That sounded like fun. Watching Isabella in action spraying her intellectual perfume and dazzling the pseudo-intellectuals gave me no gratification. I had had enough of being a beautiful drifter, a high wire dreamer, fabricator of ideas magnetic, an exotic creature. I had suffered more by not working, making my own things. I had been infected by the voyeuristic life we were living. There is a difference in rebelling against the puritan ethic of working yourself dry and working because you are having a great time creating a world that has never existed, but I went on in good faith. It was hard to believe that Isabel had just come out of the hospital. And there was a change! She was content to work at her writing, so I was content to be making her a special gift. I was making a mirror. The area for the glass was held by a figure, myself. The shape of this floating form outlined her face. I was holding her reflection.

We had a devil of a time locating a foundry and after the casting I was able to finish the bronze in a local jeweller's shop. The workers were amazed that anybody with long hair could put in a full day's work. Longhairs were 'hippies' and not expected to be productive. Isabel was delighted with the results. The next step was to have a glass cut. No one seemed able to tackle the job. I got the feeling that the Catalonians didn't like working for foreigners. This surprised me because I was in the middle of negotiations with a restaurateur to do a mural. Was it bad luck or they were too busy? I let it sit for the moment. The mirror without a face.

32

I Spent A Kiss Dreaming

Coffee in the bottle, flowers in the vase. Windows open, the morning air is fresh, it's autumn. The banker is sweeping the sidewalk in front of our bank.

I'm pouring the coffee into cups, walking into our bedroom.

"Good morning, Isabella."

The soft hazel eyes opened into daylight and into my heart.

"Good morning, Mr Gauguin."

"Very cute, I had no idea you were poetic this early."

"Oh, I had the most wonderful dream," Isabella said, "we were going on a boat excursion, down the Amazon, and instead of a jungle it was Madison Avenue."

"Wonderful."

"And guess what, darling?"

"What?"

"Everybody was cheering us because we had just come back from a triumphant tour of Europe and everyone wanted to meet the great painter."

"Come on, you're making this up as you go along."

"You're right. How's the coffee? Let me have some."

It was a great dream, even if she had just made it up.

"Got any time for me or are you going to make me a monument?"

"I'm sorry, I'm booked, I'll have to check my calendar, maybe you can have the rest of my life."

"Don't be too generous, save some for the folks outside, they need you just as much as I do."

"Seriously, want to go to Paris for lunch?"

"Sorry love, I've got to take a bath and you know how long it takes."

"Dinner, then?"

"Well, maybe, let me think about it while I soak."

"You've got a deal," I said, "press hard, Mabel, there are eight copies."

"Very funny, that's my line," she said.

There was a small gallery down the block, Isabella had noticed it. They had an exhibition of paintings based on Joyce's Ulysses. I guess the word was out. Anyway, Isabella invited the gallery owner up to see my work; he liked it and wanted to see more as I kept going. He especially liked the soft romantic nudes coming out of the ocean. Great, no problem, that was a good way for me to go. I was feeling romantic. About a week later Ira left for London and then we got a letter from him shortly after saying that they didn't let him in because he didn't have enough funds. He was now in Amsterdam and he would keep us posted. Barcelona began to look very grey and somehow empty without Ira. The travellers had moved on and then the gallery closed. Isabella and I were in good form and I had completed several paintings. We were tired of Barcelona. The question was clearly where to go. First, we had to pare down belongings. I shipped off a trunk to my sister who was now in New York, studying acting. (Later Toni was to star in a horror film she made for my father, she was fabulous. Her independent spirit however would lead her to the world of ceramics. She is a talented inventor of her own delicate world.) Sending her my own belongings lightened us up considerably. Isabella put an ad in the paper and we sold the car. Our own funds were low so we had to economise. Isabella thought that she should go to Marrakesh while I tried to set up in Paris, since that was where I was always talking about wanting to go, why not now? Was she sure she didn't want to come with me straight away? No, it would be easier for me alone to get a feel, as well as cheaper. "What if I fall in love with someone?" I asked. Isabella wasn't concerned. I began dancing around and clapping my hands. I was happy. We laughed and smiled into each other's arms. We caressed each other. Tender rolling on the bed. Hands softly touching, looking deep into each other's eyes, the rocking feelings of fullness. Looking always into each other's eyes we saw the glow of sex mirrored. Love in her eyes. I spent a kiss dreaming.

33

Paris, Let Me Swim In Your Streets Forever

Paris, Paris, let me swim in your streets forever. I was walking onto a painter's palette. Paris is noisy, refreshing. I was now 24 years old. I had to admit it to myself: I felt opened-up; not that I didn't love Isabella, but there were battle wounds and you know Paris. For the moment I had myself to myself in my favourite city or at least one of them and I was going to sing, dance, explore and if I wanted to pick up a pretty girl, well, who was going to stop me? I was forever finding another hotel near Place de l'Odéon. I felt comfortable in that area, always full of people, and affordable. Each day I headed out into the delicious autumn-winter brisk bristling to a different museum. L'Orangerie a perfect collection, and in the Modern I loved sitting in Brâncusi's studio. Recharging my batteries I saw a retrospective of Mondrian and a collection of Egyptian masterworks from King Tut's tomb. Seeing so much art and from such diverse periods, I began to also see my influences and feelings more clearly. The language of painting and sculpture defined itself through cross-reference. It was not a vacation; it was a period of re-entry.

Clearly, what was important was beauty. The beauty of colour, of form, of feeling, the fullness of it, the richness. It made no difference if it was created three thousand years ago, or three hundred, or thirty. All that mattered was that it impressed me with its beauty. And if the beauty was delicate, rough, gentle or strong mattered little. Looking at the artwork I seemed to know the man, and he had an interest in my getting to know him. He wanted to impress me with something, and that force carried the image or the shapes or whatever it was that he wanted me to feel. I felt it deeply. The world is running around looking for love, looking for fame, looking for beauty, and here it was right up on the wall not going anywhere, not needing me to complete its beauty. Yes, you could in a way add to it, invite it to meet your friends, or the other beautiful feelings you create, but it was not essential. It was a world complete unto itself and how puzzled it is at our struggle. When am I going to stop all the chasing around and just sit quietly for a while, for a year if need be, to drink in the beauty? Even a sip is renovating, cleansing, rejuvenating and filling. What does it matter if the world is topsy-turvy? If everybody would stop to have a drink of this beauty they would start to get well. I wanted to shout, to scream, to declare an international vacation. Everybody likes that word, 'vacation', and then I'll sneak them in, one by one, and give them the tour. Impossible to leave untainted by beauty. I should feel invited to camp out, open a good bottle of wine and spend a few days with Cezanne or Vermeer or Pollock, or whomever I choose. Who knows what they may have to say about geometry or physics? Certainly they are experts on medicine and they will make you well. You will walk out a new person, 'beautified', and with luck you will infect the neighbourhood, which will in turn infect the city. In a month or so the country will be inoculated. There will be an international plague. Beauty will no longer be just skin deep, it will be the whole caboodle clear through. And then we have a chance for love. And that will be that. We won't have to worry about anything. That's it, folks! That's my scenario for the cure. Well it's a fine notion anyway.

At the Museum Rodin I began by walking through the gardens, which are filled with his sculptures. Bronze, autumn-winter, cobalt skies, white cumulus, pebble path through the garden, standing at the end were two lovers embracing, embracing forever in bronze. It had been raining and there was a reservoir, a tiny pond, between the lovers. Floating on this miniature lake was a wooden house, a small red house left like a flower by a playing child or a playful poet. A young couple were now approaching the sculpture. I could see that they were in love and I was hoping that they, too, would be thrilled by this imaginary hideaway. They looked self-consciously at the two nude lovers under the tree that shaded the bronze, but not long enough to notice the red schoolhouse. I picked it up and showed it to them, laughed and put it back. Maybe they would remember later when they needed a boost, or thought of buying a house to live in.

Charting the intuitive mathematics of Rodin's language of curves, adding and subtracting the hills and valleys, the dramatic and romantic, the sensual and intelligent, the monumental and the intimate; the dance of form I saw in Rodin's meaty vision for love was both the Donatello and Michelangelo of his period and for all time.

It was time to enter Rodin's studio, a château, a single square building, beautifully placed to one side of the gardens with large windows all around the interior. The light flooded this large cathedral, making all his maquettes and plasters very visible, easy to see. What a fantastic studio; any artist would envy it.

Off to the side was a small collection of paintings, paintings Rodin had collected for his own pleasure. Among them a Van Gogh. I seem to think it was Vincent's room in Arles, one of the versions he painted. I wondered if this was one of the paintings that Theo had sold for his brother? It wasn't really surprising that an artist should have been one of Vincent's collectors and I pondered Rodin's feelings. Interesting how sculptural Vincent's paintings were. Did he ever try to make three-dimensional works? You see, Van Gogh would have made a great sculptor.

Yes, I felt good, and as I walked away from this romantic world my meeting with Jacques Lipchitz came to mind. I was a sculpture major at Bard College and I had sought out Mr Lipchitz, having needed encouragement for my own work. Researching his background I was pleased to learn he was a friend of Modigliani who had painted a portrait of Jacques and his first wife. Jacques Lipchitz would prove to be gracious to me and also deeply reinforcing. I had presented myself in front of his studio with my portfolio and a bottle of wine. He reprimanded me for bringing him wine but he did study my portfolio quite closely. Straight off the bat, Mr Lipchitz asked me if I were Jewish and if my visit meant that I wanted to become a sculptor? He said that in America I did not have to worry, I would

MEETING with JACQUES LIPCHITZ

not starve. The important thing was to understand that 'sculpture is the only morality', meaning that it would have to be the core of my existence, and if it were true, if my passion were strong, then somehow life would look after me. Of course this was more than the benediction that I had come for. Mr Lipchitz said that I should walk around his studio and look at his work and leave him alone to examine mine. It was not easy for me to relax and study his work knowing that he was looking through my portfolio.

His studio was a concrete structure sunken into the earth. It was about three thousand square feet in the shape of a square and packed with works that spanned his career, an overwhelming collection of baroque forms that were difficult to assess, being so closely placed together. Toward the back of his studio was a delicate head of a young woman, an early work, a tender portrait of innocence and very moving. There were several small bronzes individually patinated to suit their forms, delightful *tour de forces* in casting and form. Cubist masses tousling and struggling atop a woven basket turned upside down and cast as a part of the sculpture. This was a study for his Hagar! There were castings of many of his most famous works including Sacrifice, Mother and Child and Prometheus, all very powerful masterworks. Mr Lipchitz's surfaces beautifully expressed many qualities of texture that seemed appropriate to the feelings and intentions of his statements.

I returned to the front of the studio to find Mr Lipchitz still engrossed in my portfolio. I didn't imagine that a man of his stature would still be examining my collection of a dozen portrait heads, carvings and works in plaster. I was twenty years old at the time. Mr Lipchitz was not, however, competitive with my work; he could examine them freely and for as long as he wished according to his interest. I felt embarrassed that I had concluded my tour while he was still engrossed in my modest collection of images spanning a few years. What were his thoughts, I pondered, as I ducked back into his labyrinth of sculptures? I was anxious for his appraisal, happily timing my return as he closed my album. I could see he was pleased by what he had seen. I felt deeply reassured. My sculpture professor at Bard was only critical of my efforts. I was still toying with the idea of becoming an actor. Jacques, like my grandfather, who was also Lithuanian had a calming effect as well. Their wisdom quieted my nervousness, my insecurities.

After this first encounter with Jacques Lipchitz, I returned to Bard and took a nap. When I awoke I felt newborn, anxious to develop myself. My meeting with the maestro, more than any other encounter, gave me a spiritual feel of the responsibility of being an artist. God blessed me that morning behind the door of his studio on Hasting-on-Hudson.

Shortly after my visit to his studio I invite him to Bard to give a talk to the other art students. He wanted difficult questions. At Harvard the students asked him what tools he used. This infuriated him. "Ask me about my philosophies, my passions, my formal concepts. The tools have no meaning." Some of us giggled which wasn't quite the response he had in mind. I wish I had thought to ask him about Modigliani, whom he had posed for, or his encounters with Gertrude Stein or Picasso. We were all rather shy and unprepared. Lipchitz was gentle but tough minded. Surviving WW2 forged a very particular strength of character.

I asked if he could arrange for a discount at his foundry as I had been commissioned by the school to do a portrait of Emil Hauser, one of the founders of the Budapest String Quartet. He was retiring from teaching and they wanted a commemorative bronze for one of the school halls. Without a moment's hesitation he told me to ask the foundry to call him, he would arrange things.

A year later I had transferred to UCLA and Jacques was having an exhibition. He took me under his arm into the reception. Later he wrote me a letter of recommendation which secured a teaching position for me. His own struggles to survive had created a deep humanist empathy. Sharing that aspect of his being was his greatest gift or lesson for me.

34

Turner, Fuckin Turner

Back in my hotel room after a sandwich at the Select, I wrote Isabella about seeing the Van Gogh in Rodin's studio and about the red house floating between lovers. All thoughts of love now floating between myself and my muse. Bolstered up by the beauty of Paris, I began to re-examine my relationship with this mercurial diva. Her beauty, her sparkling and deep interest in life and how to live it. If her need for freedom was selfish, it also freed me to deal with love— not through feelings of possession and control, but from higher or finer areas of consciousness. Wasn't the experience of love richer that way? To share a bed without resentments and reprisals. All the feelings of being reborn or fears about making a living. Confused fears all mixed together transferred to Isabella? And the kif hadn't helped, it had accentuated these tensions, confused them. I had made some money working for Philip Yordan, so much the better. I had produced a handsome suite of lithographs, several portraits. It was up to me to push these things out into the world, rather than sitting on them as I had done. Now I was in Paris, and it was time to put myself into something that would take the pressure off, that would provide a stable base from which to operate. That was the thing to do.

I fell into a sleep feeling resolved, at ease. I was lying on the pebble beach in Capri, where I had spent the last month of a summer being the independent ten-year-old. Mornings sunning myself, waiting for the courage to build before putting the rubber tube on and going for a swim in the clear water. Sitting quietly alone, listening to the soft lapping of the waves gently slapping the morning shore. Listening to the waves and looking at my navel, thinking of meeting the Italian medical students whom I had befriended and the new songs we would sing walking up the road on the moonlit night. Listening to the waves and thinking of the young American girl I was going to see for dinner. She lived up a path. I had met her with her parents in the restaurant, the one that overlooked the bay. The same bay that I had peeked into and seen all the fish, and sea anemones opening and closing. All the fish making their way in that vast silent space that eventually disappeared into darkness. I preferred the light of day, the air, the smell of the pine trees, the soft breezes and laughter of the Italian boy scouts who sometimes played with the German boy scouts, even though they camped on different sides of the island. I enjoyed playing Fish, a card game, with the old, fragile man I had met at the plaza in town. He spoke English. And the bus driver who always took me for free. My only regret was killing the ants that morning, I must have been angry at my mother and sister. They were right, though: I should have included them in on a few of my social connects; it was very selfish of me. I never thought to ask them how they spent their days.

I was up bright and early, out into the morning to have coffee with my working class acquaintances. Everyone seemed so enthusiastic and cheerful in the mornings. The fresh croissants, the hot, steaming café au lait, the turning of the newspapers, the songs of 'Bonjour, Monsieur So-and-so' …always that high-pitched lilting intonation, always on the upswing. Perhaps I could get a part-time job at Shakespeare and Company; it might be fun working in that bookstore. Certainly it would be convenient. It was run by a quirky fellow who let it be known that he was the great-grandson of Walt Whitman.

Standing close to the stacks in the back of Shakespeare and Co. I was startled to see a figure I recognised instinctively as Jim Morrison. My heart began to jump and I walked over and grabbed a book next to him. His general manner was that of someone who does not wish to be disturbed or seen.

"What are you reading?" I asked quietly.

Jim turned and gave me a long look. We hadn't seen each other since Morocco but it was instantly apparent he knew who I was. A large grin lit up his face.

"Oh, man it's great to see you!"

Jim spoke quietly, his voice filled with affection. He turned to face me more fully.

"Isn't Paris cool?"

It was like we'd be watching a movie and had come out of the theatre to discuss our feelings. It was clear he was in literary heaven.

"You know Mike, I thought of you this morning when I went to L'Orangerie Museum to see Soutine. I thought of that painting you left at my doorstep when we were at UCLA, a thousand years ago."

Jim gave me a brief hug and then we gave each other a visual going over: we were still two scarecrows looking to uncover the face behind the voice of the Wizard, not of Oz, but reality.

"I never thanked you for that mess, maybe it helped inspire one of my songs, *The End*, 'cause in a way you are that special friend."

"Really, Jim?" Jim was being ingratiating. I doubted that he had addressed me personally in his song. Who knows the origin of an inspiration? What I did understand from his comment was that he needed some feeling of closeness just then.

"Why not? Remember that guy I brought to your apartment from Kansas? It was raining cats and dogs, and I barged in and asked you to put him up. You were the only guy I could turn to."

"God yes... Dwayne. I think he stayed on for a whole month."

"What are you doing in Paris, Mike?" Jim changed the subject.

There was a hush hush atmosphere to the bookstore and we realised we were exploding with a lot of emotion.

"Let's have a beer around the corner," Jim announced taking me under his arm.

"Right."

"I'll pay for this book. Have you ever read Rilke's poems?" Jim asked with a change of tone in his voice.

"I've read *Letters on Cézanne*, which was lovely. His poems I read too long ago to be fresh in my mind."

"Come on, let's hit it."

Jim was wearing a navy jacket and he looked like any other young American tourist.

"What are you doing in Paris?" I asked.

As we walked up the embankment along the Seine, the light

flickered on his face and Jim put on a pair of sunglasses.

"*The Doors* have had a run of success, a lot of success. I've escaped for a day. This is my reward," Jim said with a touch of glee in his voice.

"Are you all here?"

"Hell no, they are in Amsterdam, they don't know I'm here. I'll go back this afternoon. I wanted to see a few sights and get away."

It was time-out for both of us and our lives were deliciously on hold if only for this small interlude.

"Are you on tour?"

"Yeah, we did a fine show in London at the Roundhouse. A small audience, appreciative. Well, I knocked myself out. The audience was so different back home."

I was listening but some of what he said got away from me. I was so pleased to see him and hear about his success. He lived in a world so far away from the relationship between myself and Isabella.

"London is so hip, I mean elegant. Michael McClure came over and talked."

"For God's sake I know Michael."

"Do you know his play *The Beard*?" Jim asked turning serious.

"I read it a few years ago when I met McClure in San Francisco. I thought it was interesting. I used to quote from it." Roberta came to mind and our dinners at the Japanese restaurants. I had liked meeting Michael.

"Yeah, well he read some of my poems and he made some suggestions."

"That's great, Jim. It made you happy, yeah?"

"You bet! McClure is bright. We discussed poetry at some length! Yeah... he wants me to do a movie of *The Beard*, but it's too close to what I do on stage now... raising hell."

We laughed. During the pause in our conversation the waiter came over to inquire if we wanted another beer.

"I envy your work Mike. You create a world alone, quietly. Being a rock star is a lot of bullshit, nice bullshit, but you know, when the music is over I feel empty, spent, and I wonder if it really means anything. We are still in Vietnam, you know."

"I almost contacted you a few months ago. I was in Barcelona where I thought you would have had a grand time doing a happening in Park Güell, which is a fabulous surreal environment. Shit, man, got to have some fun."

Then Jim changed the subject again.

"I ducked into the Tate in London, with a terrible hangover. I wanted to see Blake's etchings but I discovered Turner. Turner man, fucking Turner. You know his portrait of Napoleon contemplating the death of a sparrow?"

I didn't know the painting then. Jim paused to visualise his experience.

"It's brilliant and so simple. Overwhelming, in fact."

He paused again to take a sip of beer before unveiling the vision.

"It's a large canvas. Golden yellow light, a huge bowl of light. Psychedelic light. In this arena stand three figures. In the foreground is a small sparrow lying on its side, in the middle stands Napoleon like a tiny puppet, you can't make out his face, he's so small. And standing further back is a soldier with a rifle. Wow!"

Jim gave a shout.

"It's the whole story of mankind, on one canvas, this is us. One shot. It blew me away!"

"Huh," I grunted. *"Plus les choses changent, plus elles restent les mêmes."*

I gave Jim a light pat on the back.

"Yeah, it sure is great to see you!"

I made some other comments about being in Spain and that I was waiting for a lady friend to show up. Mostly I was hungry to hear Jim talk, to hear about his life. And he was cheering me up as well, talking about painting and my influence.

I think he missed the old days, horsing around in Venice.

"I want to do film but I don't want the same old stories. I'm tired of being a sex symbol."

The notion of being a sex symbol was odd to my ears, especially since I had had so much trouble with Isabel. I laughed. Jim laughed for his own reasons.

"I saw Stanley Kubrick's *Space Odyssey* in London. Wow, but it's too formal for me; I want something more avant-garde."

I had seen the film in Barcelona, and I nodded as much.

"It's a perfect circle. That I did like, life to death. Do you ever think of death?" Jim asked me, the tone in his voice was easy.

"Shit, Jim, you're Hamlet; you're trying to rewrite an impossible play. I mean it, you're a kind of prince. Fuck, I wanted to be with you, but you had to do it alone. I know that now, just as I know I have to make my own way. I love you man, 'cause you were always considerate of my feelings."

Maybe I was euphoric but the essence came from a place of truth and I was happy to say it, to say it out loud.

We looked at each other. We each realised we admired something unique in the other and to acknowledge it was a good thing to do, even necessary.

"Yeah, rock is a gig. I do get off playing with the audience. I guess I make it too serious sometimes." Jim was smiling. "I like seducing them, playing with them, stretching them out, scaring them, hell… scaring myself too, ha! It's what keeps us alive, on the edge, not knowing what is going to happen. But I love them too."

I was proud of Jim. I wasn't jealous because I knew I could not do what he had done. Mostly I was happy for him.

"Look Mike, I have an idea. I'm going to record an album of my poems one day and I'd like you to add a few drawings for me. What do you say?"

"Of course, man, I'd love it."

"Tell me more about Isabel," Jim added another smile.

I could feel our encounter had come to a close, that Jim needed to move on.

"I'll write you a note."

"Yeah, let's stay in touch. You can reach me c/o Elektra Records and, ah, send me some photos of your new work, OK?"

Jim wrote down the street address on a napkin and put twenty francs on the table.

"I'm sorry old friend, but I got a plane to catch. See ya."

I got up as well and we embraced like good brothers. I watched him saunter up the boulevard.

"Give my regards to Pamela," I shouted.

Jim waved an arm without glancing back. I felt swell that at least I'd had the moment to tell him how much I appreciated his grace, something we don't always express to those who mean something to us. I'd send him photos of my lithographs; he'd like them now that we had had a beer in Paris.

Seeing Jim had made me feel good. That night I was greeted by a nightmare.

Jim was the poet, the young and beautiful poet Sebastian that Tennessee Williams had created in his play, *Suddenly Last Summer*, who is devoured by a flock of starving urchins. In my dream, Jim's fans overwhelm him on stage and become the monsters of the Goya painting in the Prado who devour people alive. I awoke wanting to understand where this vision had come from, an expression perhaps Jim had slipped into our conversation that I hadn't noticed consciously. The voice from my LSD radiator had returned to haunt me, to remind me of our cannibalism. I quickly dressed and fled what seemed like a horrible cell, not the romantic Parisian garret I had fallen asleep in. Jesus H. Christ was that how Jim felt? Now I understood another reason for his stage antics, his jumping all over the stage, falling to the ground and his drinking, it was a wall he built to protect himself. What a way to make a living.

Standing in the spaciousness of the Tuileries Gardens I thought about what Jim had said about painting, and that he wanted to encourage me, that he was sincere about his feeling about my choosing to be a painter, that he had been thrilled by Turner. The other side of his life was a nightmare: not the garden of earthly delights he sang about, that was an idealisation. What could he say to a fifteen year old girl about his ocean of joy or sorrows? He, too, must feel alone. He had given me a glimpse of his fame, a freak show that he needed to escape from, to get away from being adored, devoured. I felt privileged to be unknown, an unknown soldier, left in peace and walking towards L'Orangerie free of anyone's demands over the sea of white gravel, which acclaimed my presence with just the right touch of equanimity.

I had returned to L'Orangerie for another swim in the impressionist world. I met two American girls, one of whom was a painter. She wanted to find a place to work, and we thought it might be supportive if we went into this venture together. I must admit there was some attraction there as well. It seemed comforting being in the company of someone my own age, someone who also had the same goals as myself. We could encourage each other, very directly; a new relationship starting up on equal ground. I liked the idea. Maybe this encounter was a gift from Jim.

35

Les Deux Magots

At American Express was a letter from Isabella. As I read, several thoughts raced through my mind, touching on various feelings, both positive and negative. "Michael, I love you—I always have and I always will. How can we meet anew? We have centuries behind us, a history we have both fought hard to have. I should never want to lose that; what I want to lose is our madness and all our needs to hurt, punish and torment each other. To have our love transformed into the perfection of our dreams. No more of the suffocating jealousy and possessiveness we both had without reason because we were always bound to each other with something stronger and finer than our madness. Don't be silly and sulky. I hope you are having a wonderful time in Paris and I want to join you. You are the Poet, Prince, Friend, Love, Creator of Beauty. I am your muse; I must be with you. Landing on the sixth, Air France Flight 842. I'll be in your arms by 3:00pm. I love you, Isabella."

Paris had changed me, lightened my step. My eyes had adjusted to a world of colour, of hopefulness, of self-confidence. I was flattered by Isabella's sentiment, her understanding of our problems. I was in love again. It was unexpected, but then, I was in Paris. Isabella looked radiant when I picked her up at the airport. She seemed to have lost weight, both physical and mental baggage; she was beautiful. We both felt buoyant and tender, poetic participants travelling under the puffs of white clouds into a city she had never been to, into the gift of a light winter that kept all of Paris radiant.

Isabella was enchanted. The streets were filled with young, handsomely dressed people aglow with activity. It wasn't just another awkward street scene; people looked at us, felt us, absorbed our presence. It was done very subtly but it was done out of pleasure. There was an energy in the air. A freshness. A saluting, like Picasso's portrait for Apollinaire, standing proudly facing the passing crowd that sauntered past the garden of the church of St. Germain, on their way to have coffee at Les Deux Magots. Paris is a woman with several bouquets, several feelings for the feminine aspects, the woman's touch, that keeps the romance fresh. We saw an exhibition of Cocteau drawings and etchings. We bathed in the glow of colour standing in Sainte-Chapelle. Isabella loved discovering the small hideaway restaurants where we ate Moroccan couscous with lamb, something we had not done in Morocco. We went to watch *Un Chien Andalou*. There was a young Max Ernst and Buñuel limping with Dalí, and an angry American drunk sitting in the front row.

Even if Paris was holding us up, keeping us distracted, it was impossible for me to keep my eyes bound to her. Somehow I had outgrown my pangs of interwoven devotion; my sense of panic no longer occurred. I was delighted to have Isabella with me but I was not going to suffer the stifling of every minute shared and each glance evaluated. To avoid being victimised by falling into this trap and exhausting the freshness of reuniting, we decided to have separate rooms in different neighbouring hotels. I could also spend time with my paints that way. Isabel was interested in meeting the young painter I had thought of renting a studio with. I saw no harm in it because we had become friends and nothing more; there was nothing to hide. Isabella seemed to accept this. She was just interested in meeting another American, fine. We all had coffee at a small restaurant near her hotel. Isabella seemed satisfied and didn't find her awfully interesting, but I sensed a small burr under her saddle. I was not going to take the bait.

The room I rented was on the top floor. It was dark, even with the skylight, a genuine garret. There was a great view of the rooftops of the Left Bank. I passed several hours making left-handed drawings, an idea suggested by notes I had read in Paul Klee's diary. I was fascinated by Klee, his delicate subterranean worlds. Myths, flags, ships leaving for knocked-together shantytowns of colourful flats, a concerto for a gypsy's life. Working with my left hand I became aware of a new pleasure of watching my thoughts with a fresh eye, demanding a different sort of concentration. The process of working very clean, taking my time, nothing clever or flashy, an honest reconstruction of my model, gave me a new feeling. If this became too intense then I would loosen up with a wash drawing. I had found delicate rice paper imported from Nepal. It had odd chunks of fibre in it and was very thin. It delighted me to put a wash of colour upon it, because I could see all the way through the paper. This gave a sense of great space. I wasn't thinking of selling these works; they were my personal investigations.

I did, however, try to place my lithographs. I thought that surely if any place in the world would love them, it would have to be Paris. I went around to several of the galleries, but no dice. Out of a sense of testing I tried flogging them on the street. People were incensed by this. I was baffled. What I hadn't known was I would soon see policemen clubbing crowds of young people. I had no idea that I was living in the midst of a revolution.

We were running low on money and while Isabel read, I went out to hustle up a gig dubbing. I managed to get a few days' work and by telling the director that I was leaving Paris, I got paid straight off. They were pleased with my work but times were bad. I had forgotten about writing articles or apprenticing myself to a sculptor. Now I was looking for some fast cash, cash to eat on. Selling The Tribune was an all day affair and it earned little. I met an artist who had been working at the American Centre, doing his own serigraphs. Now he was selling papers. This wasn't for me. Riding the Métro, seeing troubadours singing, I thought I might just get down to the bottom line, stop futzing around. I made about fifteen bucks in an hour panhandling. My technique was straightforward. I got off the subway and methodically asked everyone for a franc, going right down the line giving everybody my spiel as directly and innocently as asking for directions to the post office. "I am an American stranded here in Paris, could you spare a quarter?" Flag waving came in handy. Usually everybody I asked came up with the franc. An elderly lady gave me a ten-franc note. I was taken aback by this. Anyone who says that the French are tight with their money may be right, but they are not without gratitude. Actually I was enjoying this scam; a young French girl offered to take me home with her for a meal and a lay. I probably would have taken her up on it if Isabella wasn't expecting me.

Our life in Paris had slowly slipped into living at wits' end. I was hardly conscious of my audacity, slipping into a crowded supermarket where I would fill my tweed coat with cheeses, cold cuts of various delicious varieties, and then buy a carton of milk to cover my thievery. We had also built up a substantial library of paperbacks using this same technique. It was easy to rationalize my guilt feelings having made a half-assed attempt at finding work, something substantial. Isabella's inertia made it easier to enjoy reading late into the night about the world of soup kitchens and poor souls scrambling for an existence in George Orwell's *Down and Out in Paris and London*. We joked about our shoplifting. We weren't going to pay for research. One day we would make it up to the world. We were arrogant as hell. But we were having a great time. Isabella said we were living like Henry Miller: we were living at the expense of others. Of course, this wasn't the case; Miller worked hard at writing, we were only reading. We were the young wolves stretching the fibres of morality to the threadbare strings that we rolled into a larger and larger ball. Miller had sought the refuge of the church, of petty jobs. We were cutting through this pastiche. We just took what we wanted. This was honest enough. Society should provide for artists; after all, they get everything in the end so why haggle details? We weren't being greedy—food, clothing, and a place to flop. The hotel didn't like our staying in mornings as they wanted us to give them an hour or two so they could clean. We obliged them and moved out one night. I don't think the bill was very much.

If I wanted a bouquet of flowers I just nabbed it. We were living in another world. Let the world work. We would just pick the fruit. La Samaritaine was a treat. Isabella was able to acquire the much-needed underwear and nylons and a few tubes of lipstick. I think it was the lift, the adrenalin that we were after. All in all, we were not cleaning up, we were moderate thieves, honest hunters only shooting what we could eat. We were both dazzled by the coats from Afghanistan that we saw displayed in the fashionable boutiques.

Beautiful embroidered floral patterns, lush fur, thick and seductive. These masterpieces were being sold for three hundred dollars and travellers told us that they had bought them for fifteen dollars to twenty-five maximum in Afghanistan. We toyed with the idea of going to buy a few coats. It would be a great adventure and, well, we had seen Paris. It was winter, there was fighting in the streets, how long could we continue running from one hotel to another? Sooner or later we might get caught. It was time to move on. We had some money, certainly enough to buy a dozen coats and then we could catch our breaths, return to Paris, find a normal situation in the spring, who knows? Right now, it was a question of day-to-day existence.

Coincidentally, we got a glowing report from Ira in Amsterdam. He had situated himself in a houseboat and was painting pipes, selling furniture and antiques having a great time enjoying a quaint 'hip' scene, digging the smokehouses. It wasn't exactly legal but the authorities overlooked this scene, which took place in dimly lit coffeehouses along the canals. It all sounded very clandestine and fun.

Paris was beautiful but it was square, bourgeois, strait-laced. The days of Miller, much less the ferment of Lautrec's Montmartre, the passion of the turn of the century or even of the Lost Generation of Stein's day, had long since passed the Île de la Cité. Now there was the revolution. Paris can be brutally grey, brutally indifferent. We passed our last night sitting in a small café near Les Halles. I sketched a man, a cripple whose feet were completely turned out. He sat on a bench sleeping with his cane beside him. We were waiting for an early train.

36

Walking Into A Paul Klee World

It was terribly cold in Amsterdam. Whatever dreams I had coming up on the train of going to see the Rembrandt and Van Gogh museums were frozen by the bitter, penetrating winds that forced me to stay inside. Our stay in Amsterdam was brief. Bundling up, we dodged the winds, ducking into doorways as we made our way to the houseboat. Isabella and Ira's business partner discussed our pending trip as I sketched their portraits. I had gotten into the habit of filling the pages of my notebook with images of people and buildings. At night we saw the whores sitting in their windows, small shadow box-like environments, waiting for customers. We saw a Bergman film, *Persona*, a disturbed romance of death, frozen despair. The delicate mechanism of Amsterdam, the fragile clockwork intimacy of her body was just too cold to explore, to ponder.

We took the train to Munich where we could catch the Orient Express to Istanbul. In Munich we thawed out, got our first cholera shots and had a delicious hot dog at the ever-so-clean railway station. I stopped in an art store and filled my coat with pastels, colours that I imagined I'd find waiting in the landscapes of Turkey, Iran and Afghanistan. Living on little or no money had become routine. We were stretching our cash for the coats we would buy. The money that we *did* spend was a reward for the ways we cut corners. Petty thievery and hotel bills paid with art works all added to the sense of exhilaration and a bohemian rite of passage that kept us on the move.

The train ride from Munich to Istanbul was Kafkaesque. In the middle of the night, gruff guards woke us for passport checks. During the day, we travelled through another grey world. The cities seemed empty. Belgrade was charcoal grey, gloomy, a generous sense of despair permeated an atmosphere of utter hopelessness. Even the trees looked ghostly. If we hadn't met a young artist at a café where we had stopped for a drink to cheer us up, we might have slit our own throats just to escape the intolerable loneliness. He wanted to go to America. It was the first time I really understood so bluntly the attraction. There was more life in his work than in the entire environment of the city. If we had the dough we would have shipped him out then and there. Any place would have been better than Belgrade.

Finally Istanbul! Tangiers on a large scale. We settled into a hotel near the Blue Mosque in the old section of town. It was around the corner from the Pudding Shop, where all the young travellers, the rucksack wanderers, gathered to exchange stories. The chocolate pudding was extraordinary. It was the perfect complement to the tall tales that provided the guidebook we were putting together. It was a good idea to get our international student cards. It would provide numerous discounts. There were also lots of stories of big drug busts and shootouts just around the corner. Terrible consequences for those that survived. We could listen to these tales with impunity. We had no drugs and weren't interested in getting any.

I became fascinated by the Blue Mosque. The exterior is a massive series of vaulting shapes that support a central dome. This grey complex is surrounded by a garden and a wall with small portals. Judging from the outside, the feel of the place is heavy, dreary. To enter the mosque one must lift a heavy leather flap that serves as a door. Nothing has prepared one for the softly illuminated blue grotto inside. In the distance I heard the drone of men praying, a rich and pleasant sound that traversed a sea of ancient prayer carpets. The men had taken off their shoes. I added mine to the collection. Standing on one of the thousand carpets that covered the floor—there were only carpets, no chairs—I was filled with a lightness of being as if I were standing in the middle of a watercolour by Paul Klee. The men prayed in the soft pools of light that were coming through the stained glass windows. The tones of the prayer were as clear and deep as the light passing through the cadmium rainbow of flowers and geometric shapes of the tall windows. They were stacked in three tiers between the blue tiles covered with arabesque designs. The space was immense and yet it felt intimate. Hanging from a long cord attached to the central dome was a network of tiny electric lights placed on delicate arms, arms that stretched out across the ceiling of the mosque like a stripped umbrella turned upside down. These tiny spots of light were suspended about ten feet overhead. The effect was like a blanket of stars. It was the touch of pure magic. A moment of utter transfixion.

Unlike Tangiers, the streets were broad and the activities of the city could be read like an open book. A man sitting in front of a typewriter was taking dictation, organizing the emotional thoughts of his client, reassuring him that the form of language would be suitable for his needs. There was the man who takes your photo for the student card you have been advised to get. The photo was developed on the spot magically in the large red box camera where a thousand faces have come into focus before setting out on the road to Kachistan, to Balochistan, Houchistan, Kattawallistan, to all the hidden, exotic places in the east that were waiting to greet you, waiting to roll out the red carpet. The bazaars were filled with buttons, rolls of ribbon, mementoes from past days, all laid out neatly on blankets or in small covered stalls; an endless flea market, an endless sea of used souvenirs calling out for new uses, new owners. It was a marketplace where a thousand magicians, a thousand Gurdjieffs were dyeing sparrows yellow to sell as canaries.

At five-thirty, the cry of the Muezzin pierced the walls of our hotel room. The morning broadcast was coming from the loudspeakers placed on the towers just up the road. The silence of the night had been broken and shortly Isabella and I would hear the rushing stream of cars coming down the broad avenue. All at once, the cobble-stoned boulevard would be filled with cars, the heavy, clumsy sound of old Buicks, Chevrolets from the fifties and Pontiacs all herded together and racing, rushing down the avenue like an avalanche of water turned loose over a bed of large stream boulders. It was time to get up. Time to face the neat brilliantine personality of the Turk who, one imagines, hides deceit, trickery, thievery, and murder behind his five-and-dime moustache. The moustaches were everywhere; they were a badge. They were the national coat of arms, the thick, liquorice black, waxed moustache. Every Turk had one and a pair of worry beads. He was held in constraint, his personality was homogeneous, static; a life that goes on interiorly behind closed doors. In public, he waited for business, pleasant, but masked by his moustache. This ambiance of limbo was everywhere, it gnawed at our bones. Getting a second shot against cholera, the needles seemed invisible.

We went to the Hilton. Maybe, by chance, we would find someone there to distract us, to turn things around. We met a young Irish girl. She was on her way to India to study occult medicine, to round out her education as a nurse. Julie and Isabella fell into conversation like two old school chums. Julie made an ideal buffer. I was able to catch my breath, to devote myself to my notebooks, to making left-hand drawings of the Blue Mosque and pieces of tapestry that caught my eye in the Topkapi Museum. Taking notes, I was tickled by the phallic headstones in the cemetery on the way to the covered bazaar. For the moment, there was a moratorium on our punishing each other. How fugitive our love was. Or was it a question of dependency on both of our parts? There was always hope, always a chance that things would turn around. It was easier to travel than to figure it out. It was easier to move on, hoping that the suffocating would dissipate, would be diluted by a new landscape.

We left Istanbul on a third class bus. I broke up the trip by reading a biography of Gandhi. I reflected on how purposeful his life had been unlike mine as a travelling artist. I hardly felt worthy of the idea. We were forced to stop at a tiny outpost before our final jaunt to the Iranian border. The roads had been washed out by the spring rains. It was an isolated compound of three buildings, a bar-restaurant, a bunk house and an outhouse, all the conveniences of twentieth century civilization reduced to the bare essentials. Being the only Anglos on this tour, my mind drifted to the exhausted corners of my imagination where horror stories originate. We felt trapped in the company of the humourless questioning facial masks of the Turks, who had no shame about eyeing us like birds in a cage. Their soggy fascination with our every move was impossible to avoid and I wondered how long we could tolerate their persistent gazing. Thankfully I was struck with the notion of doing a mural on the blank wall of the restaurant that was staring at us as well. Anything to energize the atmosphere. Using my drawing of the exterior of the Blue Mosque as a model, I outlined the structure over the entire length of the wall. I thought I'd be safe using such a national monument as the basic design. My goal was to fill in the geometric areas with the colouration of the inside of the Mosque. The distraction was working. I had their attention and I wasn't thinking of getting my throat slit. I tried to time the process of filling in the colours with the oncoming darkness so that I would complete the job by bedtime. The completion of the mural seemed to meet with everybody's approval. I sealed the pastels with the fixative I had also brought from Munich. It was a real touch of magic: the first spray job anyone had seen in that part of the world. One of the Turks came up to investigate the drying aerosol. For a moment I forgot myself and motioned to the Turk that he shouldn't touch the wet surface. As he respected my wishes I knew that we would all have a good night's sleep. It certainly cheered the place up. I'm sorry that I didn't take a photo of it. Maybe I forgot that I had a camera or just didn't want to expose it.

What a relief it was to be leaving the land of the thick moustaches! There was an air of pleasant intelligence that greeted us at the Iranian border. It would take almost two days crossing under the belly of the Caspian Sea to reach Tehran. The Iranian bus was more modern and I felt more at ease. The stranglehold lifted. I was able to daydream. We were passing under Mother Russia, large bowls of caviar, salmon fighting their way upstream, we were passing the meridian of Odessa, the place of my mother's birth.

It always gives me pleasure thinking about my mother. Her hands, her voice and her wisdom were always the aspects of her personality which came to mind. Perhaps it was her sense of aesthetics, which I inherited; she was drawn to beauty and passion. Her second husband was Gordon Kingman, a lawyer, I believe. She hardly ever spoke of him; he bored her. One fact about him did strike me as interesting; he was a great, great grandson of George Washington, first President of the United States. In retaliation, my mother said she was a descendant of rabbis and horse thieves, which explained her independent and self-assured manner. Her tone of voice was pleasing to my ear; it could be forceful and convincing in an argument or sweet and gentle in other moments. She always spoke to me as if I were her equal which made us friends rather than related. As a naturalized American she felt privileged at Columbia University. She received a librarian's scholarship which rewarded her with the freedom to read whenever she wanted. She appreciated that period of her life, her youth—living and struggling in Greenwich Village. She was a real New Yorker, a person who enjoyed philosophising about life's voyage.

37

Rocky Raccoon

comming to Herat, Afghanistan

Tehran reminded me of LA: low, spread out, almost nondescript, lots of traffic. The architecture was mostly European and the dress was mostly western. It takes energy to travel; passport checks, new visas, shots, exchanging monies, new surroundings and food to familiarise yourself with. Where to hang your hat and where to get a soothing shower. Sometimes, you just got to go out to play. Crossing a large square at night, a debonair gentleman pulled up in a Mercedes-Benz to enquire if we would be interested in coming to his home for a cup of tea. He has travelled to the West and would relish the opportunity to practise his English. The American abroad has the advantage of coming from the country that is almost universally seen as the great thrust into the future. There are still people who dream of finding gold in the streets. Just by being in the company of an American, the charisma of his knowledge will somehow rub off, his life will be improved. At his home we had tea and I was challenged to a game of chess with his seven-year-old son. The boy beat the pants off me. In fact, he played so beautifully that I got a glimmer of the intelligence, the clear logic that tells you how things have to be done. Chess is not a game that is won with charm; it is not a game of luck. It is a game of logic methodically applied. It is ironic that the Persians could play this game so well and yet be so easily caught by the emotional upheavals that were to follow in their history.

Isabella and I were in love with the fresh yoghurt. It had a wonderful texture imbued by the green ceramic cups, the returnable bottles, as it were. The atmosphere was considerably lighter in Tehran. I met an American school teacher who seemed quite happy. She missed certain things but basically liked her lifestyle. The heavy defeatist quality of the Turks was even more apparent now and exploring Tehran we felt better about everything. How easy it was for us all to adjust to circumstance or to lose track of how we wanted to live and where.

Isabel met a young American jock with a VW van who needed gas money. He was going to Afghanistan. For a moment we were back in the twentieth century listening to the just-released Beatles record, *The White Album*, on a tape cassette. Rocky Raccoon in Iran. On the road to Tabriz it occurred to me how wonderful it was, how unique and comforting to hear the Beatles, always upbeat, always cheering one on. How special it had been to have heard *Hey Jude* in Barcelona and now *The White Album* in Iran. Finally we were approaching the border to Afghanistan. The guard was dressed in an old American army coat and was wearing a turban. He stood by a small guardhouse that looked English. He seemed very pleased to see us and asked, "Food, chai (tea), or hashish?"

We were drifting into Afghanistan.

We travelled across a bumpy road for some time and then we were greeted by the ruins of an ancient temple awaiting us from behind a cluster of pine trees. Deep cobalt tiles of lapis lazuli glowed in the sunlight on a dome that was half-cut away revealing the interior of the structure. The tiny pine forest protected this sentinel, which lay at the top of the dirt road that drifted down into Herat. The road was also lined with Italian stone pines that arched overhead; there were miniature bungalow stalls that displayed radiant groupings of dyes and other substances that could not be identified without closer inspection. It created a joyous bouquet of colours. It was like a series of large jewel boxes, the tops thrown back in anticipation. Children ran alongside our van shouting, "Goodbye, goodbye."

Later, thinking of The Beatles' *Hello, Goodbye*, I wondered if they weren't fans as well.

All of Herat is constructed of the same khaki-coloured adobe structures. All except for the bank, which was a deep emerald green and could have passed as native to any Mediterranean environment. The feel of Herat struck us as being very peaceful. The people were friendly and gentle. The women wore long robes, completely hiding themselves. These hooded gowns made me think of a cloth version of the visors worn by Teutonic knights; only the pupils were visible.

The American jock was a real pain in the ass. Now that we were in Herat we could split up. We wanted to be alone. The village was absolutely charming. Isabella and I took a ride sitting under the canopy of a phaeton. We trotted through the town to a lovely park. Things were peaceful between us again. It had taken two months to get to Afghanistan. The trip seemed to have affected our moods. Travelling from grey winter cities to the warm, friendly village of Herat, the landscape had become more and more uplifting and lighter and lighter in tonality. We had travelled into the light from the dark.

Back in town I was approached by a man who wanted to know if I were Jewish. He said that Jews had been living in Herat since the time of Alexander the Great. He wanted to know if I would join him for a cup of tea. Of course I was delighted to meet him and the other five men who were all probably descendants of the original tribes. They spoke a simple English, enough to enquire where I was from and where I was going. I explained that I was from California, an artist, and that I had come to Afghanistan to buy coats; they were popular in Paris and I wanted to get the best quality. They suggested that I go to Kabul, the capital. They wished me luck and added that I should go to the museum there; I'd enjoy the art. I bid them farewell, thanking them for their hospitality. How wonderful to have been treated so warmly, so directly. I liked Herat just then; there was a sense of softness, a kind of cousin to wisdom, an ambience of welcome: do what you want, feel at home, we greet you with kindness and open arms. For the most part, the Afghanis lived in a twelfth century world. This rudimentary existence had a certain seductive charm. I wished I could bottle some of its raw energy, the open naïveté. Unfortunately, it's very hard to separate from a culture trying to internationalise itself. These qualities undergo a certain subterfuge. They are caught to some extent by artists who try to capture these nascent characteristics, so wonderful to experience in their original forms.

The ride to Kandahar was a full day of jostling up and down on metal seats. In the distance were huge mountains whose tops emerged beyond the horizon of a carrot-coloured desert. They seemed to be watching us; they looked like large cyclopean monsters. The terrain was flat, desolate, not a traveller in sight. We were exhausted by the time we arrived in Kandahar. The village seemed to raise right out of the earth just as the sun was setting. Only our hotel distinguished itself with a wash of white colour, otherwise the buildings blended right into the earth. There were very few trees and the buildings were one storey high. The colour of the village seemed bleached out in the desert sun. The men wore robes and the women wore veils revealing little more than the women in Herat.

In the hotel we heard the sound of organ music coming from one of the rooms. The music was Western and modern, somewhat Satie and Bach. We were informed by the hotel clerk that it was one of the guests, a traveller who had secluded himself in his room for months and that he did not wish to be disturbed. This guest was pursuing his education, as I was mine. Each experience, each encounter, added another glaze to the finishing of the vase. The most mundane aspects of reality seemed to suggest certain lessons, and there seemed to be always something delightful about the truth. The following day, walking around the silent, almost invisible village, we came to the banks of a river where a horse was drinking in the brown liquid. Further down women were doing the wash and in the distance we could see a man urinating into the water. We drank only hot tea or bottled liquids. Coke was available. It's spelled differently in Farsi but it tastes the same. Isabella liked the red kerchiefs but we didn't buy any. Kandahar is off the beaten track. Julie, Isabella, the mysterious European and I were the only visitors in town. Most tourists fly directly to Kabul from Herat. In those days the trip cost ten dollars. We couldn't afford it.

38

Readymade Planet

Coming into Kabul the first omen to greet us was a European crossing the street with his pet monkey at the end of a long leash. This welcome to the capital suggested to me that it would be okay, that everything would go smoothly. The man and the monkey were a cheerful talisman; maybe it reminded me of how I met Errol Flynn. This town was considerably more modern than Herat. There were a few cars, several hotels and a movie theatre playing an Elvis film—it had been dubbed into Farsi but the songs were in English. We found a cheap hotel up a dirt road off the main plaza. Our suite was on the top floor at the end of the hall. We paid about twenty-five cents a day for the room. Outside our window was a view of the native quarter, brown cocoa buildings, terraces, trees and laundry accenting the landscape like pieces of colourful paper. The buildings drifted lazily into the distance just below the foothills. Kabul is surrounded by mountains. Paul Klee in ochre colours or an early Mark Rothko watercolour.

There were a great many men wandering around town wearing turbans and long American army coats. Some of the native women were wearing miniskirts. Random bits and pieces of western civilization had found their way to Kabul. The variety and incomplete aspects of this phenomenon delighted us. Wherever we went the food was the same—dumplings and sour cream sauces. We stayed away from meat. There were several travellers in town, all very friendly and helpful. Several had come to this enchanted locale via India. This was of special interest to Isabella and Julie. Isabella thought that she would continue on to India, being so close and all. In the beginning, we more or less kept to ourselves. I was doing a lot of drawings and watercolours, views from our window.

One morning on the way to the jewellery bazaar I noticed a man selling rocks. Stream stones washed down with oil. He had selected the oval shapes. How wonderful! The stones had been collected from the Kabul riverbed, which was a few feet away under the bridge we had just crossed. The man understood the secret of leaving nature alone to perform her own magic. The artist needs only be able to see beauty. It wasn't necessary to recreate it. I thought of Marcel Duchamp's metaphors, which were merely more sophisticated but the naked truth was the same—readymade. Further down the road was a group of men surrounding a vendor selling eggs. The eggs were all dyed a bright fire engine red and the vendor was tapping one egg against another. There was great excitement about this activity. Some eggs were getting more attention than others. This ritual had no meaning for us but it suggested several possibilities: gambling, testing the eggs for freshness, or testing to see if there were any chickens about to pop to life. I never did find out.

In the bazaar we found a few handsome examples of antique Afghani necklaces; flat silver diamond shapes made a screen which was decorated with carnelian stones. We couldn't resist buying them. They were very inexpensive. There were no coats in this bazaar; they had to be sought out on the other side of the town. That area proved to be more cheerful. It resembled the small bungalow stalls we had first seen coming into Herat but these were larger. One walked into the shops up a narrow path. On each side of this path were coats piled one on top of the other. The coats had not as yet been cured. After going through shop after shop, perhaps ten in all, we discovered that the gold rush was over. The best coats were already in Paris. There were still some beauties, but not too many. Even if we had travelled halfway around the world we didn't have a lot of cash left, so there was no harm done. Finally we selected four coats: two were full length, one had white fur and red embroidery, and the other was charcoal with a curly Karakul inside and some black detailing. The remaining two were short jackets. I think we got the best four coats left. The boy whom we did business with was a tough little tyke. He wouldn't give an inch in his price and he never cracked a smile; business was business. Prices had gone up a couple of bucks. It wasn't *The Treasure of the Sierra Madre*, but at least we had a few coats and our whole lives ahead of us.

We could be lighthearted about our adventure. I felt we had gained many emotional insights which were more valuable than the small cash profits we thought we needed. Looking out over the soft, dull, khaki brown landscape disappearing into the foothills of the surrounding mountains, I felt a decompression of being.

I saw flags of laundry symbolizing my conflicts. They were now cleansed and drying in the spring air. Seen at a distance these dancing colours flying at different angles allowed me to separate myself from what had seemed like very important issues. I felt a sense of pleasure, a plug had been pulled and I could give up the notion of being important, it was OK to be a painter. The poetic delights I had been collecting now all came together, a chord inside me sounded like a visual orchestra. The minutiae, the minor details of experience; the red wooden house afloat in the rainwater in the lap of Rodin's bronze lovers, or the sudden flash of electric colour in the undergarments of the women I had seen in Essaouira. These visions also had dignity like the young women wearing a Goya outfit crossing the street in Granada. These were the elements I could put to good use in building my studio. This was the world where these songs could be reconstructed or presented properly. This was the theme I was building like the tiny bird I had been so struck by, who had insisted I hear him out and it was a fantastic repertoire… these were the treasures I would be bringing back. I had made a kind of idiotic tempest in a teapot, but I could forgive myself. And I could embrace my father whose very overcoat had been my knobby co-conspirator providing me with an endless pocket where hidden food, pastels and books had gifted my journey, just as his actions had inadvertently given me my Italian experience. I wouldn't have done it alone, without an audience, and Isabella had pushed me.

Knowing that I would be leaving soon, I decided to go out one morning on a sketching tour, hoping to capture something special. I headed out in the direction of the coat bazaar but I took an unfamiliar route. In passing a small park I saw a wonderful burly tree. The baroque botanical dance appealed to me. It was a really mad piece of nonsense and I got so deeply engrossed that I was unaware of a crowd of children that had gathered behind me. As this madman stepped back to study the tree and his drawing, the children began to giggle. When I showed them what I was doing they howled with laughter. I motioned for them to stand still and turned to face them, trying to capture their expressions. They kept laughing and were not at all interested in stopping to hold a pose. I singled out one of the faces and drew rapidly. When I showed it to them they were still laughing, laughing and waving goodbye. It was like trying to get the attention of a flock of birds.

There are special moments one experiences when the mind at peace slips a fresh roll of film into the mental projector. Turning a corner, continuing my stroll, I was almost aware of this form of consciousness. I came upon a small sign posted on a wall. Painted in blue letters on a small wooden plaque it read: Swami Boobala. A small arrow pointed to the right. The name amused me, a Jewish swami, so I followed the arrow. At the next corner I noticed another sign and so I continued, my mood aroused to another ascending pitch of enthusiasm; I didn't question the pleasure. Over a simple pink door was an eye painted within a circle. Surely this was the entrance to the swami's home. Before knocking I had the sensation that I was to experience a special interview, not some foolish trick. I don't know where this intuition came from but I took the moment seriously just as I had when I visited Jacques Lipchitz's studio. I knocked. The door was soon opened by a woman with a pleasant face.

"Welcome," she said and gestured with her hand that I should enter.

"I am an American," I said.

"I speak English," she said. "Come, I will present you to the swami. What is your name?"

"Michael. Thank you."

At the end of a small hallway I was ushered into a pleasant room; windows faced each other, illuminating the space, lending an uplifting quality to the environment. Sitting at a modest table was a man wearing a turban. His face was neither young nor old and was free of pain or any forced expression.

"This is Michael," the woman said.

"Come in, young man." The swami chuckled. His laughter put me completely at ease. It brought to mind the wonderful laughter I would hear over the radio which belonged to Alan Watts.

"Sit down, please... I will get a sense of you without words." The swami's face had a relaxed expression and yet I felt as I sat facing him that I also faced a mirror of a sort. The reflection of what might be perfect about my soul, as if somewhere within my being was a sealed package, now to be opened by the swami. I felt that he knew that I knew; he was merely reaching for the ribbons. The room took on a glow and I laughed from embarrassment.

"This is normal, Michael. You are letting go of the outer shell. I see it is easy for you. What is your profession?"

"Swami Boobala, I am a painter!"

"This is a perfect profession for you. You are fortunate to be able to make beauty. This is a fine way to embrace your love. It is a pity that everyone is not taught painting or music, or dance or theatre, for each of the arts brings people to themselves and each other. To keep the child within us alive! The product of art is less important; it is the experience of the making or the doing which teaches you to breathe."

The swami laughed. It was a lovely sound which filled this diminutive room.

And I laughed as well, now feeling quite comfortable. I could sense the swami would now convey a deeper philosophical truth, that he had paved the way.

"People come to me following their own path. I do not teach and I have no followers. I put up my sign when I sense I will be receiving a guest. You, Michael, are my guest this spring. You have a special gift and you have a special life, a life of freedom, in freedom. One day you may have the opportunity to help many people. And many will help you. We all have a kind of programme to follow, a certain day, a lifetime to fulfill. Your gift will have to do with beauty and grace, qualities of balance and understanding, compassion... very special qualities when they are pure and complete. Remember one thing, humility is your honey, and with it you will not fail your potential. The ego is man's greatest enemy, it blinds him from the truth which is his true grace. Do you have any questions for me?"

Without thinking, I said, "Will the world ever live in peace? Will wars stop?"

The swami gave a chuckle which seemed inappropriate.

"The world is a place of conflicts, of survivals. But we are intelligent enough to make peace possible. It would profit the world a great deal more to live in peace. You will play a role in this. And whether or not a lasting peace will be achieved in your life or the lives of people as a species is only a matter of willingness and sharing. Each day is a new chance for this reality to be made. Perhaps a new road must be taken, where being right or wrong is no longer the issue. To be different is good, not evil. What beliefs one follows are only valuable if they provide the believer with inner peace which is expressed and shared. It is time for peace, which seems to take a long time. But it is always time for laughter and song."

The swami put his hands together in prayer and laughed as if to seal the experience.

"Go in peace, Michael. Forgive everyone; it is only their limited thoughts which bother you. Each heart is pure inside if beating. Be happy you are a painter, a maker of beauty."

We sat for a moment in silence. I felt healed, purified and I also knew that I'd probably keep this experience to myself. Something for my own garden.

"Thank you, Swami Boobala, for a most exhilarating experience."

"It is a gift for you! Treasure yourself and treasure life. That is all you can do! The rest will follow."

I walked away in a state of pleasant reverie. My life with Isabella was an exotic dance. It had lasted from our meeting in Madrid in April to that moment a year later when I waved goodbye to her as she got on the bus with Julie to India. We parted as friends that April morning and why shouldn't we have? It had been a crazy affair but we had done things together that I know I never would have done alone. In a way it was a kind of second period of teenage rebellion, of stretching the boundaries of human psychology, our own and those around us. I wasn't sure that I would ever see Isabella again and it really didn't matter. We had spent thousands of hours together pushing and pulling all the strings, touching all the bases, all the dreams. We knew each other, we thought, as thoroughly as we knew ourselves. We had shared an umbrella of delight like the tiny lights hanging as a sea of stars in the Blue Mosque... we had shared the box of iridescent delicacies which all lovers invent praise for and a love for each other stripped bare of artifice, we thought down to where the chemicals sparkle. Rarely do these poetic moments sustain a romance. Like all experience its beauty may be short-lived. These infatuations—the wild flowers that bloom in spring, their colours so fresh in the crystalline air—soon fade as the heat of summer begins to announce itself. Our fault lay in the fact that we simply never made our nest. The perfume of freedom was stronger for each of us.

The whole cosmos is travelling, pushing into the black space. We sit on this blue orb with white brush strokes sorting out endless conflicts, nuances and inventions. From outer space none of these problems are visible, we see only a beautiful blue/white planet floating in a black space. If we could view our problems with objectivity, at a distance, we might find that beauty could help us. The purity of the blue waters of earth and the white of our clouds offer a standard of keeping it all clean and running smoothly. The value is in the beauty of this chemistry set... what we build with it can be anything. I opened my bosom to release a cry of exhortation... LOOK HOW BEAUTIFUL IT IS THIS LIFE. WHY CAN'T OUR SOLUTIONS BE AS BEAUTIFUL AS FRESH AIR?

My obligation would be to paint from my heart. My goal would be to acquire a balance in my being, to use modesty with an honest tone. To be more appreciative of each breath. It was a tall order but I was feeling good, new born, awakened as from a wonderful nap.

39

A Passport For Jim Morrison

On my return visit to Herat I shot my last roll of film. One of the small children that I photographed was on the truck which took me out of Afghanistan. She was with her guardian; she was a very pretty little girl. I had the feeling that they were hoping I'd take her with me to Europe or wherever I was going. I wonder what has happened to her since the war?

Foolishly, I had drunk some water in Kabul. By the time I was on the bus going through Turkey, I had become quite ill. The bus driver seemed in a panic to get to Istanbul and refused to stop. It was painful and embarrassing sitting there smelling up the place but there was nothing I could do about it. I sat there as dignified as possible reading *Naked Lunch,* cursing the Turks with my farting and apologizing to my fellow travellers. By the time I arrived in Istanbul, the yoghurt I had eaten in Tehran had settled my stomach. The chocolate pudding put the finishing touches on things. Luckily, I was able to use my Pan Am ticket to fly to Paris. Up in the plane, I caught a glimpse of Greece. The cobalt/ultramarine Aegean looked so peaceful that I wished I could have dived in.

In Paris, I sailed through customs. I had braved taking a few chunks of hash with me. Had I been caught in Iran or Turkey, I might still be there today, but there is an angel looking over me—a very forgiving angel. It was a big relief to be back in the West. And Paris is always so beautiful in the spring. She has a way of welcoming me like no other city. Walking up rue M. Le Prince once again I happened into a record store. Joni Mitchell was singing *Michael from Mountains* and I saw the cover of a new *Doors* album. There was my friend, Jim, saluting me. I had really been out of touch; there was so much to catch up on.

After a light meal I decided to turn in early. Back in my room I thought it would be nice to have a hit of hash. I hadn't had a puff since Afghanistan and I hadn't smoked very much of it there either. I lit a cigarette and placed a small chunk on the burning tip and then sucked up the thick smoke through the empty cartridge of a ballpoint pen. My chest felt light and I quickly drifted into a deep sleep. In my dream I found myself walking around Paris. A man whom I seemed to recognize as Jean Cocteau was directing a movie, which I was apparently a part of. Cocteau was pleased with the way things were going. He said that he wanted this scene played quickly as if the action were double time. Cocteau waved his hand to signal 'action', but I was startled by the bright lights necessary for filming.

Ahead of me was a group of people that I was to observe as they approached. Stepping to the side, I got a glimpse of a person that I thought I recognised as Jim Morrison. As the group passed I was to shout, "Hey, Jim, how's about an autograph for an old friend?" at which point the actor replied, "Sure, meet me here tomorrow, same time." Cocteau's choice of actor was idiotic: he was too fat to be Morrison and besides he had a beard. However, my reaction for the camera was supposed to indicate that I had said something stupid, that I felt disgusted with myself for trying to get his attention with such a banal and unoriginal remark. We had to re-take this scene several times because I couldn't seem to react the way Cocteau wanted me to, but this didn't seem to disturb Cocteau, either. In my dream we broke for lunch and then returned to work. The following scene took place as indicated at the same spot. Again, Cocteau waved his hand and the lights went on. In the dream I was now approached by another actor who was thinner and who had no beard. He bore some resemblance to the Jim Morrison I remembered and when he read his lines he sounded just like Jim.

"Glad to see ya. Follow me. Don't say anything."

Cocteau was very pleased and was applauding. But this new impersonator had disappeared. I ran after this phantom. We entered the subway and got on the train. Instead of the empty tunnels outside the windows, I saw a film. The movie was about a rock star but we never saw his face. The scenes didn't last long either. The actor was reading a book. I saw the title: *Time of the Assassins*. It's a paperback by Henry Miller on the fate of Rimbaud. The actor looked up from his book smiling. Each time he did this, the scene in the movie changed out in the tunnels.

All at once, Cocteau appeared on the set, only this time he was upset. He yelled, "Stop, stop, very bad, méchant, bad, boys." As I was apologizing to Cocteau, Jim slipped away, but I got a glimpse of him walking by the subway window. "Make-up, make-up," Cocteau was saying, which made no sense to me and I left in pursuit of the company of the person pretending to be Jim, who I enjoyed listening to thinking this must be the real Jim. I was now running down a street trying to catch this fellow whom I was yelling to.

"Jim, Jim, wait for me!" He darted around a corner but I was catching up. At the corner Jim somehow was now much further along. In fact, he was ready to disappear again at the head of the block. It was futile for me to continue and I started to cry. Now a figure had its arms around me. I looked up. It's Morrison.

"Michael…"

"Jim."

We embraced and then he asked me if I happen to have my

passport on me. I said no, that it was back at my hotel.

Jim exploded: "God, fuckingshitfuckcuntfucking God, can't you ever get your lines straight?" This upset me, and I said that it wasn't my fault.

Then he replied, "This is my life and I want it for myself; can't anyone understand a simple fact like that? I'm tired, besides I'm supposed to meet Isabella in Nepal."

"You're a fucking liar," I said, "You don't even know Isabella." At which point Jim started crying.

Then I said, "Look, Jim, I'll draw you a passport. No one will ever know the difference." Jim liked that idea and we decided to have a drink over it. Laughing, we were now having a good time. I confessed that I was doing a monument for his grave. Jim said I should send him a photo when it was completed.

40

There Are No Goodbyes

I was startled by the idea of his death. It was very early in the morning and I awoke in a cold sweat. I didn't want to go back to sleep so I got dressed and went for a walk. Paris was beginning to stir, single notes of sound broke the night's silence. I thought of the composer John Cage. One of his concerts consisted of him merely sitting at a piano in silence. The corner bistro struck the final note, the sound of a spoon rapidly placed on a saucer announced they were ready for their morning customers. As I huddled over my steaming café au lait, I thought back to my dream. It was an awful dream. Jim and I were the same age, twenty-five, it was unlikely that he would be dead. Was Jim famous? What the hell is fame? Was fame like a good brew of coffee, waking me up that morning? It's easy in Paris. It was a convenience to walk into a café au lait like walking into a great performance; it was all in a cup. All I had to do was drink it. What the hell is fame? Something like a doggy-bone? That's for history. It's a convenient tale you tell to make a point for a history book.

Drinking my café au lait I was also thinking of the foolhardy mistakes I'd made, and that's what it was to be twenty-five. Dammit, it didn't matter. It was all in the past. I thought Spain would give me something, and it did. It gave me the feel of Spanish dignity, Goya, etchings, lithographs, wonderful Greek Dimitri and his enthusiasm for my being an artist. I wasn't an actor, that was my father's trip, and he had done it brilliantly. If he'd fucked up, that was okay, too; it added to his mythology. It was time for me to have my own idiosyncratic fencing duels with life. They were all in front of me, an airplane trip away, back to America, back to my homeland. The world of art had amazed me, delighted me, now it was my turn. I had to make a dance, make a ride, make something that was mine.

It was time to develop what I could claim for my own fame. Fame is, after all, a question of merit. I could see no reason for not leaving. I'd get in touch with Jim. It would be interesting, and I could do lithographs for his lyrics. God, there were so many possibilities, all I had to do was to go make them happen. I'd get a studio in New York, I'd dig in, I'd paint my adventures, the people, the landscapes, yeah… it would be fine, I was heading home. All I had to do was to go.

Coda

Yes, I did go back home, to dig in and continue my life as an artist. I did several exhibitions and a few in the right places. There are some curious stories in these adventures pursued with high hopes and concocted under Chaplinesque circumstances. My lone wolf days in Venice, California and subsequent romance in Barcelona had the advantage of taking place in a time which now seems more innocent. Revolution was well intended. I felt I had more freedom of time to explore even the ridiculous. The pleasure of making art, however, has grown, and that involvement with creation has paid off with a great deal of self-satisfaction.

That is a realistic achievement I can expect for myself and pass on as inspiration. Sometimes when I'm very quiet I can sense Jim with me, just like the moment in Venice when I thought that Shakespeare had popped by for a visit. Well, the imagination is a grand thing.

In my imagination there are no goodbyes.

About The Author

The extreme exoticism of the painter, sculptor and writer Michael Lawrence's path through life began at an early age.

He was born in Los Angeles in 1943 to the Hollywood character actor Marc Lawrence and the screenwriter, poet and novelist Fanya Foss. When Michael was 7 and his sister, Toni, 3, the family moved to Rome after his father had become embroiled in the Hollywood McCarthyism scandal. There, Michael's childhood home became a magnet and natural melting point for Italy's own film community and the film-makers, writers and actors of 1940s Hollywood passing through. This heady mix of Outsiderism, defined by Felliniesque beauty and surrealism, fame, genius and the traumatically self-exiled, emotionally distant, father, famous for playing "baddies" from Ziggy in *Key Largo* in the 1940s to several *Bond* villains, provided a rich foundation for Michael's art. His first watercolour sale, at age 13, was for a pound to the Welsh actor and film producer Sir Stanley Baker. They'd first met in Rome when Michael was visiting his father on the set of *Helen of Troy*.

After returning to the US as a teenager, Michael studied art at UCLA. There, the formative years of dropping out and tripping with college friend Jim Morrison were followed by the award of a Huntington Hartford Fellowship. This, along with the encouragement of his mentor, the Cubist sculptor Jacques Lipchitz, and his vibrant, intellectual mother (amongst other accolades, she was the New York representative of Ford Madox Ford's *Transatlantic Review*), had Michael's future set as an artist and writer. His first article, on LSD, *Like Swift Death*, was published in the *Los Angeles Free Press* in 1966.

The influence of Lipchitz is evident in Michael's art, which brings together a unique, direct line of influence from the two great Bohemian periods of the 20th Century: the 1920s Montparnasse group of Lipchitz, Gris, Picasso and Modigliani, and the birth of the 1960s Alternative Culture which Michael experienced at such close quarters. After avoiding, along with his friend Jim, the very real threat of conscription to Vietnam, another famous friend, Roy Lichtenstein recommended Michael for a Krasner/ Pollock Grant, describing his work as "vibrant, joyous and colourful". Michael didn't get the grant, but by then he was on his way. He has had numerous one-person exhibitions in Los Angeles, Palo Alto, New York City, Denver, Madrid, Stockholm and Greece.

For the past 22 years Michael has lived on the Greek island of Hydra, an outpost of the art world, painting, sculpting, writing and swimming. His works can be found in hundreds of private collections internationally, including those of Oliver Stone, Eileen Getty Wilding, Moderna Museet, LA County Museum of Art and the libraries of Bard College and MoMA New York. His artwork has appeared in several films including *The Royal Hunt Of The Sun* (1969), *The Strange Exorcism of Lynn Hart/Pigs* (1972/1984) and *The Doors* biopic directed by Oliver Stone (1991). Other writing includes profiles of Spanish artists for the *Castiliana Hilton Magazine* and performance pieces *An Evening In Paris* (1984) and *Modigliani In Florescent (1978)*.

> *"A privileged life. Would that every child could experience such richness, a formidable education... a very strong humanist landscape... like John Lennon's IMAGINE song."*
> Michael Lawrence, Hydra, 2016

Other titles by Michael Lawrence

My Voyage in Art (fast-print.net 2014)
Loaded Brush (fast-print.net 2016)
The Sexual Life Of Bread (Blackbird 2016)
Modigliani In Florescent (Private printing 1978. Reissue, Blackbird, 2016)

Keep up to date with all Michael Lawrence news, join the
Michael Lawrence Mailing List
(All email details securely managed at Mailchimp.com and never shared with third parties.)
http://eepurl.com/bEFmV9

Michael Lawrence's website
www.worksbymichaellawrence.com

Further Reading

No One Here Gets Out Alive – The Biography of Jim Morrison by Jerry Hopkins and Danny Sugarman (1997, Barnes & Noble; first published 1980, Plexus)

The Sheltering Sky by Paul Bowles (Penguin Modern Classics 2004; first published 1949, John Lehmann)

If you have enjoyed this book, would you consider leaving a short review at Amazon.com; Amazon.co.uk; Waterstones.com (UK) or www.barnesandnoble.com (US)? Online reviews really do make all the difference to the life of a new title. Thank you.

If you would like to know more about becoming a **Reader Ambassador** for *Tripping With Jim Morrison & Other Friends* please email us at editorial@blackbird-books and we'll let you know how you can become a valuable, visible, part of this book's journey to a wider audience

Reader Ambassadors

Anne Porter
Kathy Porter

745 Washington Street
New York, New York 10014

December 11, 1991

Michael Lawrence
918 N. San Vincente Blvd.
Los Angeles, CA 90069

Dear Michael,

Dorothy and I were happy to see slides of the survey of your energetic, joyous and colorful work.

I will be happy to do Pollack-Krasner and the Gottlieb foundations when they send me the forms. (Sometimes the Krasner people have just called me.)

I won't try to compete with you in the word department except to say how much we enjoy reading yours.

Dorothy joins in sending best wishes. We are glad to hear that you are so well.

Best regards,

Roy Lichtenstein

http://blackbird-books.com
@Blackbird_Bks
#authorpower
Discovering outstanding authors

blackbird

www.ingramcontent.com/pod-product-compliance
Lightning Source LLC
Chambersburg PA
CBHW020611300426
44113CB00007B/600